More
Adventures
with Kids
in San Diego

San Diego County

More Adventures with Kids in San Diego

Adventures in the Natural and Cultural History of the Californias

A series edited by Lowell Lindsay

Judy Goldstein Botello
Kt Paxton

SUNBELT PUBLICATIONS
San Diego, California

More Adventures with Kids in San Diego

Copyright © 2001 by Sunbelt Publications
All rights reserved. First edition, 2001. Second printing, 2003.
Printed in the United States of America

06 05 04 03   5 4 3 2

Address all correspondence to:
Sunbelt Publications, Inc.
P.O. Box 191126
San Diego, CA 92159-1126
619-258-4911 • fax 619-258-4916
www.sunbeltbooks.com

Edited by Jennifer Redmond
Book design and composition by Robert Goodman
Cover design by Leah Cooper
Maps, illustrations, and cover photo by Russel Redmond
Photos by Victor Botello, unless noted

Library of Congress Cataloging-in-Publication Data

Botello, Judy, 1943-
 More adventures with kids in San Diego / by Judy Goldstein
 Botello, Kt Paxton;
 [maps and illustrations by Russel Redmond].
  p. cm.
 Rev. ed. of: Adventures with kids in San Diego. c1991.
 Includes index.
 ISBN 0-932653-45-6 (pbk.)
  1. Outdoor recreation for children--California--San Diego
County--Guidebooks. 2. Family recreation--California--San Diego
County--Guidebooks. 3. San Diego County (Calif.)--Guidebooks.
I. Paxton, Kt II. Botello, Judy, 1943- Adventures with kids in San
Diego. III. Title.

GV191.63.B69 2001
796-5'09794'98--dc21   2001032774

Contents

Maps

Central San Diego

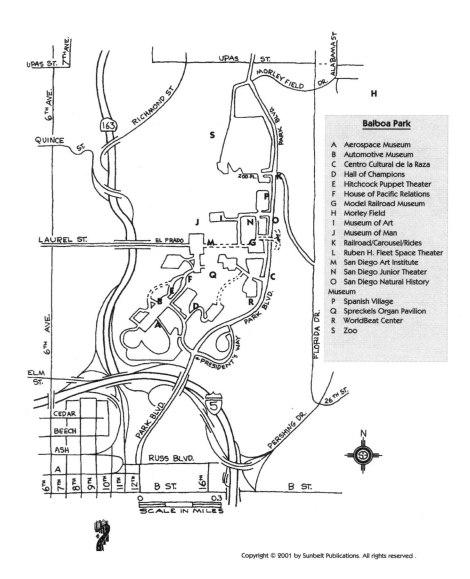

viii

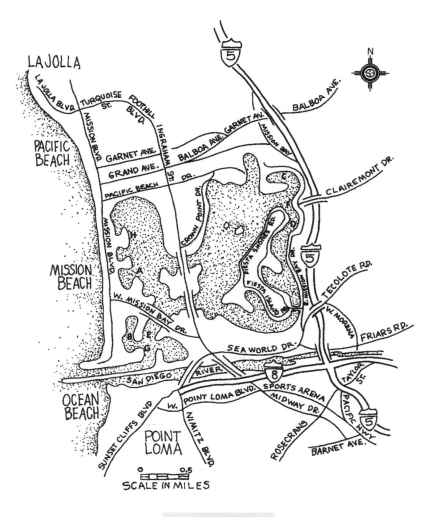

LA JOLLA

PACIFIC BEACH

MISSION BEACH

OCEAN BEACH

POINT LOMA

LA JOLLA BLVD.
TURQUOISE ST.
FOOTHILL BLVD.
MISSION BLVD.
INGRAHAM ST.
BALBOA AVE.
GARNET AVE.
MISSION BAY DR.
BALBOA AVE.
GARNET AVE.
GRAND AVE.
PACIFIC BEACH DR.
CROWN POINT DR.
CLAIREMONT DR.
FIESTA ISLAND RD.
FIESTA ISLAND RD.
MISSION BAY DR.
TECOLOTE RD.
W. MISSION BAY DR.
W. MORENA
FRIARS RD.
SEA WORLD DR.
SAN DIEGO RIVER
POINT LOMA BLVD.
SPORTS ARENA
MIDWAY DR.
TAYLOR ST.
SUNSET CLIFFS BLVD.
W. POINT LOMA BLVD.
NIMITZ BLVD.
ROSECRANS
BARNET AVE.
PACIFIC HWY.

N

0   0.5
SCALE IN MILES

Mission Bay

A   Bahia Point
B   Bonita Cove
C   De Anza Cove
D   Leisure Lagoon
E   Mariner's Point
F   Mission Bay Visitors Center
G   Mission Point
H   Santa Clara Point

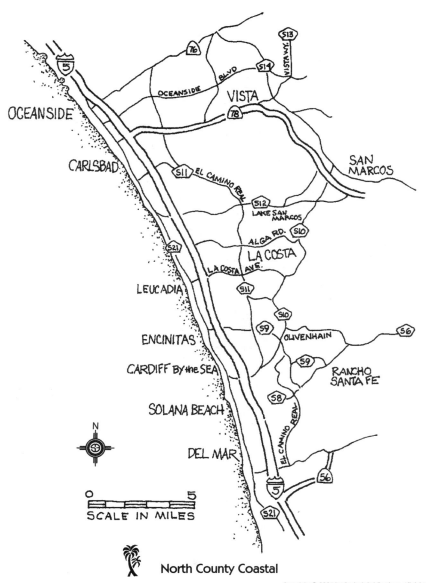

North County Coastal

SCALE IN MILES
0   5

x

 South County

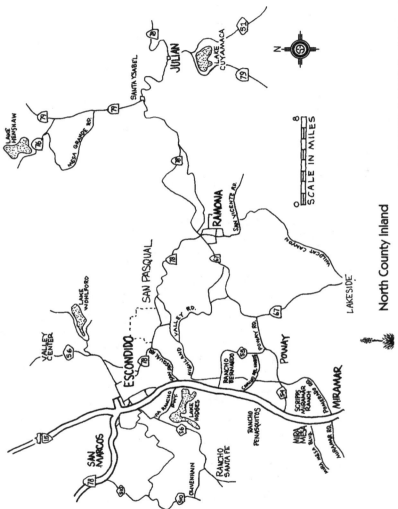

North County Inland

SCALE IN MILES

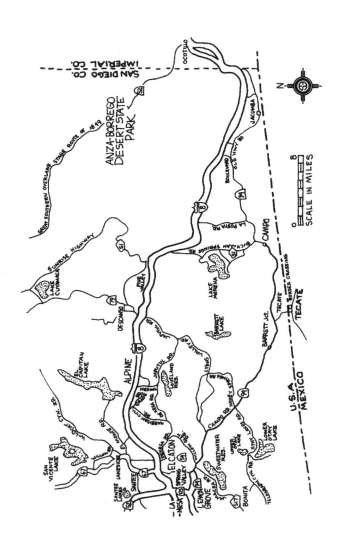

ANZA-BORREGO
DESERT STATE
PARK

SAN DIEGO CO.
IMPERIAL CO.

East County

SCALE IN MILES

N

Introduction

☆ Judy...

When the first edition of *Adventures with Kids in San Diego* was published in 1991, my own kids were just emerging from their childhoods, transforming themselves into young adults. San Diego, too, was transforming itself—leaving behind the overgrown small town that my children and I had enjoyed and emerging as the rich, vibrant and diverse county that I now enjoy with my grandchildren.

Such has been San Diego's transformation over the past decade that this new edition of *Adventures with Kids* is more than twice the size of the original. Every chapter includes attractions that didn't exist ten years ago. Many attractions now offer websites—virtual adventures—that were undreamed-of in 1991. But perhaps the most exciting addition in *More Adventures with Kids* is the voice of my co-author who, as the mother of two young children, brings a real-life, down-to-earth perspective to every adventure.

Without Kt Paxton—my co-author, my daughter, and one of my best friends—there would be no second edition of this book. Her enthusiasm, imagination, and unflagging dedication illuminate every page. To her, and to my granddaughters, Sabrina and Casey Paxton, I owe a deep debt of gratitude. They have kept alive in me the spirit of fun that was the driving force behind *Adventures with Kids* ten years ago; and they have helped me reconnect to the abundant riches of our region. We hope our readers will have as much fun exploring San Diego as we did.

☆ Kt...

When I was first approached to update *Adventures with Kids in San Diego,* it took only half a second for me to look at my Mom with complete disbelief and cry, "Are you crazy?!" I was handing my four-and-a-half year old her snack with my 18-month-old attached to my hip. I was in the process of doing ten loads of laundry, there was a stack of ironing sitting in front of me, and the breakfast dishes were waiting in the sink. Between diapering my baby and sweeping the crumbs from snack time, I said, *"If* I could find the time"—and that seemed like a big *If*—"what do I know about writing a book? Forget it. Thanks but no thanks." I spoke emphatically. And that was that. Or so I thought. However, the more I thought about it, the more fun it sounded. I also thought that with a little encouragement (and a bribe of seeing more of her grandchildren), my mom could co-author the book. My Mom and I had always had a close relationship, and I knew that this experience would either drive us closer together or drive us crazy! I am happy to say that the men with the white coats have yet to come to either of our doors.

In fact, we've had fun together and we complement each other nicely. My co-author is very "outdoorsy" and has many outside adventures to share. However, my oldest daughter, Sabrina, is all girl and doesn't like to get dirty—her idea of an adventure is trying on flower-girl dresses at the local bridal store. I knew I had to get my two cents in and remind my mom that there are great adventures inside as well as outside.

So, I would like to take a minute to thank my co-author, Judy Botello, without whose encouragement, support, and hard work I could have never finished this project. I would also like to thank my kids, Sabrina and Casey Paxton, and my husband, Scott Paxton.

And remember, if you have kids in your life, everyday is an adventure. Enjoy it!

☆ How to Use This Book

San Diego County covers a lot of territory, both geographically and in terms of the kinds of adventures available. Our hope has been to make this book useful, practical, and informative; to that end, we'd like to offer a few tips to help our readers get the most from More *Adventures with Kids in San Diego*.

❀ The book is organized into ten chapters that are loosely arranged around areas of general interest. For example, if you are a San Diego resident expecting out-of-town guests with children, you might consult Chapter 1 ("The Big Ones") and Chapter 2 ("Balboa Park"). If your family is particularly interested in sports, or if you have a vigorous adolescent who needs outlets for his/her energy, you might turn to Chapter 9, "Adventures of the Body." Perhaps you have a budding artist, actor, musician, or scientist in the family—read through "Adventures of the Mind," Chapter 8, to find out what the community has to offer. A son or daughter studying history in school could lead a family to some "Adventures in Time," Chapter 7.

❀ The general geographic region of each attraction is always indicated in the text, and the Appendix lists all of the attractions by region. If your main interest is finding adventures with kids that are not too far from your home, consult the Appendix under "Adventures by Region." We have chosen to divide the county into five main geographic areas: North County Coastal, North County Inland, San Diego, East County, and South County. This division has required us to make a few arbitrary decisions, and while some might argue whether Vista is coastal or inland, or whether Ramona is North County or East County, we've tried to use our best judgement. The major communities that we include in each area are as follows:

- **North County Coastal:** Oceanside, Carlsbad, Vista, Leucadia, Encinitas, Cardiff-by-the-Sea, Solana Beach, and Del Mar.

- **North County Inland:** San Marcos, Escondido, Ramona, Julian, Rancho Bernardo, Rancho Peñasquitos, and Poway.

- **San Diego:** The area bounded on the north by Mira Mesa and Scripps Ranch, on the west by La Jolla south through Point Loma, on the east by Tierrasanta south through Encanto, and on the south by Golden Hill and City Heights.

- **East County:** Santee, Lakeside, La Mesa, El Cajon, Lemon Grove, Spring Valley, and all points east to the Imperial County border.

- **South County:** Coronado, National City, Chula Vista, Imperial Beach, and all points south to the Mexican border.

❀ Most of the listings in the book include a price, or a price range, or—at the very least—a telephone number to call to get the price. In the Appendix, we have included a section in which we list all the attractions in our book that are **free**. Thus, if cost is important to you (and who can say that cost isn't important!), check the Appendix for those adventures that will cost no more than the price of the transportation there and back.

❀ The one way by which we have *not* categorized attractions is by age. This was a decision born of a good deal of discussion and many years of experience with kids. We feel that there is just too much variation among, say, 4-year-olds, or 10-year-olds, to generalize about which attractions will appeal to which age groups. You have to know your child, and you have to use common sense in planning your outings. (For example, most 4-year-olds have shorter attention spans than most 10-year-olds, although there are exceptions!)

❀ One of the most important bits of advice we can offer readers is to **always call ahead to check** on current prices, schedules, etc. We have made every effort to present information that is accurate and up to date, but these things change so frequently that it is always wise to confirm.

❀ Throughout the book, you will find personalized tips from "Mom" (Kt) attached to the page with a paperclip...

or from "Grandma" (Judy) attached to the page with a clothes pin.

This is our way of sharing with our readers the very real adventures that we've enjoyed as we've compiled our information. They are the tips we offer to our own friends and family as they set out to explore our special part of the world, and they come from the heart. But the final words of send-off for any adventure with kids are the best ones of all: HAVE FUN!

❀ By the very nature of this book, the information in it is always changing. We would love to hear from our readers about adventures we've left out, information that is no longer valid, or new attractions that we've not included at all. Please feel free to send us your comments, suggestions, and experiences at our e-mail address: adventureswithkids@hotmail.com. We look forward to your input.

Judy Goldstein Botello
Kt Paxton

The Big Ones

It is the premise of this book that, for the most part, you need not spend a fortune to enjoy a special adventure with your family. However, there are a few San Diego family attractions that are so famous, and so much fun, that we could not possibly leave them out, despite the fact that they are pricey. So here, in the first chapter, we will deal with San Diego's "big ones"—those adventures that will set you back a few dollars but are worth it. These are, for the most part, the attractions for which San Diego is best known.

THE SAN DIEGO ZOO
(San Diego)

619-231-1515 or www.sandiegozoo.org; 2920 Zoo Drive off Park Boulevard. In Balboa Park, just north of downtown San Diego.

Admission: Adults $18.00; Children ages 3-11 $8.00. Children 2 and under are free. Admission includes access to all exhibits and shows. The 25-minute guided bus tours, as well as the aerial Skyfari ride, cost $5.00 for adults, $3.00 for children ages 3-11. A deluxe admission, which includes both the bus tour and the Skyfari ride, costs $26.00 for adults, $14.00 for children ages 3-11. Parking is free. Zoo membership, which allows for free admission to both the Zoo and the San Diego Wild Animal Park, as well as discounts on bus tours, costs $76.00/year for 2 adults or $60.00/year for 1 adult. Koala Club membership for children ages 3-15 is $19.00/year and allows for free admission to both parks, and discounts on bus tours, as well as discounts on all special events and classes. During the month of October, all kids are admitted free!

Hours: The zoo is open 365 days a year. From September through May the gates open at 9:00 A.M. and close at 4:00 P.M. From Memorial Day to Labor Day the gates open at 7:30 A.M. and close at 9:00 P.M.

When out-of-towners think of San Diego, they are likely to think first of the world-famous San Diego Zoo. Its fame is well deserved: Its wonders are as delightful for parents as they are for children. The Zoo covers about 100 acres of canyons and mesas, and includes about 800 species of animals. Obviously, seeing it all in one day is impossible. After a few leisurely visits,

Some children, especially those under the age of 6 or 7, may be bored with the bus tour and the Skyfari, as they do not offer direct experience of the animals.

Be aware in the Children's Zoo that although the little goats, sheep, and deer are small and gentle, they may be larger and stronger than some little people, and bags of peanuts or other food items clutched in small hands are an invitation to the animals to help themselves!

you and your children will develop favorite spots and favorite animals; at that point, a trip to the Zoo becomes more like a visit to old friends. But for the newcomer or the tourist, the 35-minute **guided bus tour** is an easy way to get a good overview of about 80% of the park. An alternative way to get an overview of the Zoo is in the **Skyfari,** an aerial tramway that affords a spectacular view of all the surrounding area.

For young children, the **Children's Zoo** is a must. Goats, sheep, bunnies, and guinea pigs welcome all the petting you and your children can offer. Baby animals peer back at baby humans through the window of the nursery where they may be seen playing with dolls, drinking their bottles, and having their diapers changed.

There are always special shows at the Zoo, and there are often animal rides that are a thrill for children. Check at the information booth just inside the entrance for times and locations. The zoo rents **strollers** and provides many snack bars

Don't try to see the whole zoo in one day! You and your children will enjoy the experience much more if you take it a little at a time.

and restaurants for hungry adventurers. If you have the luxury of being able to see the Zoo during the week, you will avoid the crowds, especially during the summer months when it can be very crowded.

During the summer, the San Diego Zoo hosts several special events that allow you and your family to see the animals in a different light (literally!). Morning Zoo Rise, Nighttime Zoo,

Kindernights, and Safari Sleepovers all offer a view of the animals at their most active. Call the Zoo information phone number above, or check out the Zoo's website at www.sandiegozoo.org for detailed information of upcoming events.

THE SAN DIEGO WILD ANIMAL PARK
(North County Inland)

619-234-6541 or 760-747-8702. Recorded Visitor Information: 760-480-0100 or www.sandiegozoo.org/wap; off of San Pasqual Valley Road (Highway 78), east of Escondido.

Admission: Adults $21.95; Children 3-11 $14.95. Children 2 and under free. Admission includes all exhibits and shows, as well as the Wgasa Bush Line train, a 55-minute guided tour through the park's "back country" where the majority of the animals roam. During popular seasons at the Park, the lines waiting to board the Wgasa Bush Line can be long, and a "preferred boarding ticket" can be purchased for an additional $4.00 for riders ages 12 and over, $3.00 for riders ages 3 to 11. Parking costs $3.00 per vehicle.

A 2-Park ticket can be purchased for $38.35 for adults, $23.15 for children 3 to 11. This covers one visit each to the Zoo and the Wild Animal Park within a 5-day period.

Annual membership prices are the same as those listed above for the San Diego Zoo; one membership covers admission to both parks. During the month of October, all kids are admitted free!

Hours: From September through May, the gates open at 9:00 A.M. and close at 4:00 P.M., except during the month of December when the Festival of Lights is in progress and the park is open until 9:00 every evening. From June 16 through Labor Day the gates open at 9:00 A.M. and close at 9:00 P.M.

The temperatures at the Wild Animal Park can be the highest in the county during summer months. Bring plenty of sunscreen, water, and hats for everyone; or come late in the day when the sun is lower in the sky.

Although it lies thirty miles north, the Wild Animal Park is technically part of the San Diego Zoo. Its atmosphere is quite different, however. The Wild Animal Park is dedicated to providing habitats as close as possible to those found in the wild for over 2,000 animals, most of them native to Africa or

Asia. The animals roam freely over the 1,800-acre park; they are separated from their human spectators by unobtrusive moats and unseen barriers. Through this natural environment, the Wild Animal Park has had great success in breeding many endangered species.

From the point of view of a child (or parent), the Wild Animal Park has a smaller, more personal feel to it than does the Zoo. The center of the Park is known as **Nairobi Village**, and is designed to look like an African fishing village complete with thatched buildings and a man-made waterfall which kids find fascinating. The small lake is home to scores of local ducks who are always ready to be fed by young visitors. In Nairobi Village there is also an **animal nursery** where baby animals can be seen playing with the same toys that their human counterparts love. Next to the nursery is the **Petting Kraal**, where gentle young deer and goats can be petted and fed.

The best way to see the animals in the Park is on the 55-minute tram ride aboard the **Wgasa Bush Line**, free with the price of admission to the park. This excursion covers a 5-mile circuit throughout which zebras, giraffe, rhinos, elephants, antelope, and many other creatures can be observed roaming free.

All kids love the **gorilla exhibit**, which provides an "up close and personal" view, and the spider monkey exhibit next to **Thorntree Terrace**, a source of endless amusement to children and parents alike. There is a small restaurant with outdoor tables near the spider monkeys,

Like the bus tour at the Zoo, this tram ride will probably not hold the interest of children under the age of 7 or 8, as the experience is not direct enough to engage them.

Butterflies are attracted by bright colors. If your youngster wears something bright to the Wild Animal Park, the butterflies are more likely to pay a personal visit!

and it makes an ideal spot to take a break. The **rainforest** exhibit is full of free-flying butterflies to delight children of all ages.

There are several hiking trails through the park, and they afford another way to view the animals. A giraffe feeding station along the **Kiliminjaro Trail** provides an opportunity (at selected times) to have a giraffe literally eating from the palm of your hand. Many a 3-year-old now knows the color of a giraffe's tongue (purple!), thanks to an afternoon at the Wild Animal Park. **Strollers** are available for rent at the Park's entrance, so very young visitors can ride the trails, if need be.

Many of the animals are at their most lively after the sun goes down, and during the hot San Diego summers, the same is true of many people. Besides the regular bird and animal shows that occur during the day, there are often special shows at night. Call, or check at the entrance for up-to-date show schedules. The Park also offers **"Roar and Snore"** overnight campouts for families from mid-April through October, and **Sunrise Safaris** during the hot month of August, when early morning is the kindest part of the day. Call the Park for details.

SEAWORLD (San Diego)

619-226-3901 or www.seaworld.com; SeaWorld Drive off of I-5 (exit on SeaWorld Drive and turn west).

Admission: Adults $39.00; Children 3-11 $30.00. Children 2 and under free. Admission includes all attractions and shows. Annual passes allow for unlimited admission and free parking. They cost $74.95 per year for adults and $59.95 for children 3-11 and seniors 55 and up. Parking is $7.00 for cars, $9.00 for RVs. During the summer, one admission ticket acts as a free pass on Thursdays for the rest of the summer if you enter the park after 4:00 P.M.

Hours: From September 5 through June 16, the park opens at 10:00 A.M. From June 17 through September 4, the doors open at 9:00 A.M. Closing time varies with the season and the day, and you should call the park for details. In general, SeaWorld is open until 10:00 or 11:00 at night through the summer months and closes at 5:00 or 6:00 during the "off season," but with extended hours on weekends.

SeaWorld is on the coast, and temperatures can often be fifteen or twenty degrees below what they are just a few miles inland. Even if you leave home on a sweltering summer day, bring sweaters or light sweatshirts for a comfortable day and/or evening.

SeaWorld, one of San Diego's most famous attractions, is another day-long adventure. Every member of the family will find something enchanting here. There are a number of shows, the best known of which is the **Shamu Show** where trained killer whales perform in a giant pool. Virtually all children love Shamu; this show, like all the others, lasts only twenty minutes and holds the attention of even the pre-schoolers. Older children will enjoy SeaWorld's ever-changing shows and great family entertainment.

11

In addition to the shows, there are a variety of exhibits, many of which are "hands on." In the **California Tidepool** exhibit, children can reach in and pull out starfish and other marine creatures. At Rocky Point Preserve, children can **feed the dolphins**, an experience that is a thrill for all age groups.

The animals are hungriest early in the day, so Rocky Point might be one of the first exhibits you'd want to visit.

In the **Penguin Encounter** exhibit, hundreds of Antarctic penguins waddle and slide like so many comedians over simulated snow and icy water in their enclosed Antarctica. The **Shark Encounter** is another not-to-be-missed exhibit: Even very young children respond to the huge sharks in their giant tank, often only a hand's breadth away from their human observers.

The local seagulls have figured out where they can get a free meal and can be aggressive in trying to snatch a fish out of small, unsuspecting hands.

At most of the shows and on several of the rides, you have a very good chance of getting wet! If the weather is not super warm, you might want to pack some dry clothes for your children.

A recent addition to SeaWorld is the **Wild Arctic** attraction, which falls somewhere between an exhibit and a ride. Guests start out on a simulated helicopter ride. Following a simulated "accident" that strands you in an Arctic landscape, you will move into the exhibit area where walrus, polar bears, seals, and beluga whales swim and surface in a startlingly realistic habitat. **Shipwreck Rapids**, a fast-paced raft ride, justifies SeaWorld's new identity as SeaWorld Adventure Park. The new **Mission Bay Theater** features special family films related to sea themes. Admission to the theater is included with admission to the park.

During popular times of year, you will need to get to some of the shows at least twenty minutes before they start in order to get a seat. Younger children may grow restless with the wait, so bring along a book or other activity to keep them occupied.

When your children are tired of shows and exhibits or when you need a break, head for **Shamu's Happy Harbor**. It's a child's fantasy playground, complete with several "oceans" of brightly colored plastic balls for youngsters to "swim" in, trampolines, climbing towers, swinging wooden bridges, and water games for hot days. Some San Diego families buy annual passes to SeaWorld just to be able to enjoy this playground throughout year.

Like the Zoo and the Wild Animal Park, SeaWorld offers a number of "special experiences." One of the most intriguing is the **Dolphin Interaction Program**. A child must be at least 6 years old and at least 44 inches tall to participate. The experience, guided by one of the dolphin trainers, lasts 90 minutes and costs $125 ($105 for annual passport holders.) Advanced reservations are recommended. Call 1-877- 436-5746 for further information. **Behind-the-Scenes Guided Tours**, also lasting 90 minutes, are available for $8.00 for adults, $7.00 for children 3 to 11 and seniors 55 and up. Call 1-800-380-3202 for further information. At the same telephone number, you can receive information about SeaWorld's **Sleep Over programs.**

LEGOLAND
(North County Coastal)

760-918-5346 or www.legoland.com; Lego Drive in Carlsbad (I-5 to Carlsbad, exit Canon Rd. and go east to Lego Drive).

Admission: $32.00 adults, $25.00 children 3-16, seniors 60 and up.
Parking is $6.00 for cars, $8.00 for RVs and campers, $12.00 for "preferred parking."

There are several options for annual passports, and their prices vary with the number of people covered by the passport and with the features included. The "Primo" passport includes free parking and no blackout dates; the less costly Block Party passport is not valid during weekends or during the summer months and does not include parking. Annual cost of a Primo passport is $99 for an adult and $79 for a child or senior. Annual cost of a Block Party passport is $69 for an adult and $49 for a child or senior. The per-person cost decreases with increasing numbers of family members included on the passport.

Hours: LEGOLAND opens at 9:00 A.M. from mid-June to Labor Day. The rest of the year, doors open at 10:00 A.M. Closing time varies with the season. During the summer months, the park closes at 9:00 P.M.; during winter and spring holiday seasons,

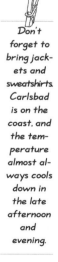

Don't forget to bring jackets and sweatshirts. Carlsbad is on the coast, and the temperature almost always cools down in the late afternoon and evening.

the park closes at 7:00 P.M. Otherwise, closing time is 6:00 P.M. in the spring and 5:00 P.M. in the winter. Call for specifics.

Check out height requirements on rides before making promises to smaller kids. Someone is often available at the park entrance to supply your child with color-coded wrist band based on his/her height. Your free park map indicates each ride's height requirements with the same color code; you'll know immediately who can ride on what, thus avoiding disappointments.

LEGOLAND is one of San Diego County's newest attractions, and it is unique among theme parks. Covering 128 acres, LEGOLAND comprises nine separate areas, each of which contains its own rides, activities, shops, and food. After being welcomed by a 9-foot dinosaur built entirely of LEGOS, families can head for their favorite attractions. **The Village Green**, oriented toward the toddler and preschool crowd, includes a boat ride through familiar fairy-tale landscapes, an interactive water play area, a "DUPLO" play area (DUPLOS are large LEGOS designed for very young children), and two theaters featuring puppet and magic shows. Older kids enjoy **Fun Town**, where 6- to 12-year olds can drive their own small autos along miniature roads complete with stoplights, road signs, etc. Junior drivers between 3 and 5 years of age can putt-putt little cars around a safe track. There is also a "Skipper School" where young captains can pilot their own boats around a small lake, and a "Flight Squadron" of LEGO airplanes. **Miniland** features LEGO replications of five "typical" American scenes including New York City, New Orleans, Washington DC, a New England Harbor, and the California coast. Each scene, constructed entirely of—you guessed it—LEGOS, includes countless intriguing interactive possibilities. For example, you and your children can push a button and start an elaborate parade in front of the White House, or strike up the band in a New Orleans street. Other areas include **Castle Hill** where you can pan for gems, ride LEGO horses, and enjoy live entertainment; **The Imagination Zone** which functions as an interactive learning center; **The Ridge** with a labyrinth to explore, and the "Kid Power Tower" offering a spectacular view from the top and a thrilling free fall back down; and **The Lake**, offering a floating tour through the heart of LEGOLAND for the footsore and weary. (Sights along the way include LEGO versions of The Eiffel Tower, Mt. Rushmore, the Taj Mahal, and other international landmarks.)

Rides, most of which have height requirements, include several roller coasters, and LEGOLAND's newest ride, **Aquazone**, a powered water ski ride. Play areas include **The**

Hideaways, an area in Castle Hill with rope climbs, nets, and intricate slides, as well as several "DUPLO" play areas for the younger crowd. Throughout the park and throughout the day, you will find all sorts of shows—puppet shows, live action shows, interactive shows—which make a nice break from the walking that you will do to cover even half the attractions.

LEGOLAND does not allow food or drink in the park. However, there are food stands everywhere, and the food is particularly fresh, healthy, and good—unusually so for a theme park! There are **lockers** available for rent just inside the entrance, and **strollers** are also available for rent.

A final note about LEGOLAND: It offers one of the best websites we have come across, including a number of pages for kids to interact with. You might want to visit either before or after you visit the park itself; the "cyberpark" will enhance your experience of the real-life one.

CHAPTER 2

Balboa Park

One of San Diego's most cherished landmarks, Balboa Park truly has something for everyone. Whether you are a lover of the arts or sciences, of history or sports, of nature or urban architecture, there is a special treat awaiting you within the peaceful lawns and walkways of Balboa Park.

Some of Balboa Park's attractions charge an admission fee (although **note** that many of the museums are free one Tuesday of each month.) But imagine a sunny Sunday afternoon of sailing leaf-boats in a pool beneath a splashing fountain while strolling jugglers and mimes entertain and the music of a free organ concert fills the air. Such hours are some of the finest a family can spend in San Diego, and although they are priceless, they don't cost a dime.

The reflecting pool in Balboa Park

Location: Balboa Park is in downtown San Diego between Pershing Drive to the east and 6th Avenue to the west. Easiest access is off of Interstate 5; take the Pershing Drive exit if you are headed south on I-5, and take the Park Boulevard exit if you are headed north on I-5. Follow the signs to Balboa Park. There are a number of free parking lots within the park itself, and parking is sometimes available along Park Boulevard.

General Information: Balboa Park Visitors Center 1549 El Prado or website www.balboapark.org. Call 619-239-0512, or stop by the Visitors Center between 9:00 A.M. and 4:00 P.M. seven days a week. It is located in the House of Hospitality, adjacent to the Casa del Prado, and offers maps and information on all Park activities, as well as a list of museum free days.

The biggest challenge in Balboa Park is deciding where to start. We have found that our favorite Park activities have evolved and changed as our children have grown. There are attractions for all ages, and you will never run out of new experiences in this rich environment. Below is just a partial sampling of adventures with kids in Balboa Park. Your family may very well discover something we haven't even thought of!

FOR SMALL FRY

☆ Playgrounds

There are two playgrounds in Balboa Park. One is in **Morley Field**, in the northeast corner of the park off Pershing Drive; the other is in the **Pepper Grove** picnic area off Park Boulevard. The Pepper Grove area also offers barbecues and picnic tables in the shade of the old pepper trees.

☆ Miniature Railroad, Carousel, Butterfly Ride

These three attractions are all located **just outside the Zoo entrance** off Park Boulevard. The carousel dates from 1910 and is as charming as they come. The miniature railroad features open railroad cars pulled by a one-fifth-scale locomotive for a 3-minute ride, and the butterfly ride (a kind of mini merry-go-round) is exclusively for the under-five crowd. **Admission** is $1.25 for each ride. **Hours** vary with the season; call the Visitors Center (see above) for current hours.

☆ Marie Hitchcock Puppet Theatre

(619-685-5045)

This is an indoor theater in the **Palisades area** next to the Automotive Museum. It features a number of different forms of puppetry (hand puppets, marionettes, ventriloquism, etc.) performed by a variety of artists. Productions change weekly. **Show times** are Wednesday through Friday at 10:00 A.M. and 11:30 A.M. and Saturday and Sunday at 1:00 P.M. and 2:30 P.M. **Admission** is $3 for adults, $2 for children under 12. Imagine the thrill of seeing and interacting with "live" puppets for a little one whose sole experience of this art has been on a TV screen!

FOR LARGER FRY

Museums

Many of Balboa Park's museums sponsor classes for children, in addition to their regular and special exhibits. Check Chapter 8, "Adventures of the Mind," for details on classes for all ages. And don't forget to check your favorite museum for summer day camps when school's out: They're educational and fun!

☆ Aerospace Museum

619-234-8291 or www.aerospacemuseum.org; 2001 Pan American Plaza. Open daily 10:00-4:30 (Call for extended summer hours.). Admission: $6 adults, $5 seniors, $2 children 6-17; under 6 free. Free admission 4th Tuesday of each month.

Stroll through the entire history of aviation, from vintage bi-planes to spacecraft. (The most famous of the vintage planes is a replica of Charles Lindbergh's "The Spirit of St. Louis.") Families can watch a real plane take shape by stopping in the museum's basement where workers are building "real-life" planes for future exhibits. There are also periodic model-building events for model enthusiasts.

☆ Automotive Museum

619-231-AUTO (619-231-2886) or www. san-diegoautomuseum.org; 2080 Pan American Plaza; Open daily 10:00-4:30 (Call for extended summer hours). Admission: $7 adults, $6 seniors and active military, $3 children 6-15. Under 6 free. Free admission 4th Tuesday of each month.

The automotive museum's permanent display features classic cars and classic motorcycles, as well as futuristic automobiles. Special exhibits often include rare vehicles. Authentic "live" restorations are ongoing.

☆ Hall of Champions Sports Museum

619-234-2544; 2131 Pan American Plaza (in the Federal Building). Open daily 10:00-4:30. Admission: $2 for every-one. Free admission 2nd Tuesday of each month.

Do you have a sports fan in your family? He or she can test his/her physical ability in the interactive Center Court area. The Breitbard Hall of Fame is the biggest attraction in this mu-seum, but there are a number of other permanent and changing exhibits as well.

☆ Model Railroad Museum

619-696-0199 or www.sdmodelrailroadm.com; 1649 El Prado (in the Casa de Balboa, lower level). Open Tuesday-Friday 11:00-4:00, Saturday and Sunday 11:00-5:00. Admission: $4 adults, $2.50 seniors, students, and active duty military; children under 15 free. Free admission 1st Tuesday of each month.

This is one of the largest collections of model trains in the world. Kids and adults will enjoy the permanent exhibit depicting historic San Diego and the railroad lines along the northern coast and south into Tecate. Special exhibits are constantly changing; call for current information.

☆ Museum of Man

619-239-2001 or 1350 El Prado (under the California Tower). Open daily 10:00-4:30. Admission: $5 adults, $3 children 6–17, $4.50 seniors; children under 6 free. Free admission 3rd Tuesday of each month.

Curious about our earliest human ancestors? Interested in other cultures, other times? This museum's permanent displays will take you on a journey through time and across the globe. Especially relevant to San Diego families is the exhibit on the Kumeyaay people, some of the original inhabitants of what is now San Diego. Among their current-day descendents, the Kumeyaay language and culture still survive. The Museum of Man periodically sponsors special events that feature Kumeyaay dancers, singers, and basket-makers.

The Museum of Man also offers a kid-friendly **Children's Discovery Center** where youngsters can explore ancient cultures in a hands-on, interactive manner. The Discovery Center costs $3 extra and is open Monday through Friday, 1:30–4:30 and weekends, 10:30–4:30.

☆ Ruben H. Fleet Science Center

619-238-1233 or www.rfleet.org; Plaza de Balboa (near the fountain). Open Wednesday through Sunday 9:30-9:00, Monday and Tuesday 9:30-6:00. Admission: The Center includes hands-on exhibits illustrating scientific principles, a SciTours simulator ride, and an IMAX theater that doubles as a planetarium. Admission prices vary between $5 and $11 per person, depending on your age and what you wish to include in your visit. Call for specifics; children under 3 are free. Free admission 1ˢᵗ Tuesday of each month. (Note: Free admission to the exhibit galleries does not include free admission to the shows in the IMAX theater.)

The exhibit galleries are virtually all hands-on and interactive, and they change frequently. Principles of light waves, sound waves, meteorology, human perception, computer science, space travel, and much, much more come to life at the push of a button. The IMAX theater changes its shows regularly; call for current information.

On the first Wednesday of each month at 7:00 P.M., the Center's resident astronomer turns the IMAX theater into a planetarium and presents a program called "Through the Telescope," pointing out current features of **San Diego's night sky.** After the presentation, the San Diego Astronomy Club gathers outside the Center with a stunning array of telecopes—some homemade—and cheerfully allows the public to check out the cosmos. If you have a budding astronomer or astronaut, in your family, don't miss this event!

☆ San Diego Natural History Museum

619-232-3821 or www.sdnhm.org; Plaza de Balboa (on the opposite side of the fountain from the Ruben H. Fleet Science Center). Open daily 9:30–4:30. Admission varies based on traveling exhibitions; children under 3 free. Call for information. Free admission 1ˢᵗ Tuesday of each month.

The San Diego Natural History Museum offers volunteer opportunities for teens. It's a great way to get some experience and to fill leisure hours

If you have a dinosaur lover in your family, this is where you can find the real thing. Dinosaur skeletons, whale skeletons, and exhibits of local flora and fauna make up some of the permanent exhibits here. There is also a wealth of hands-on classes

The San Diego Natural History Museum offers a special Grandparents' Membership!

for little naturalists, as well as field trips for the whole family (See details in Chapter 8, "Adventures of the Mind.")

☆ San Diego Museum of Art

619-232-7931 or www.sdmart.com; 1450 El Prado. Open daily Tuesday through Sunday, 10:00–4:30. Closed Monday. Admission: $8 adults, $6 seniors, youth (18–24), and active

duty military, $3 children 6–17; children under 6 free. Free admission 3ʳᵈ Tuesday of each month.

Art appreciation comes naturally to children; it is only as we grow up that we learn to be intimidated by the word "art." At this museum, you will find a gallery of animals created out of wire, stone, and other media that will delight everyone. The Art Museum schedules periodic **Sunday Family Days** throughout the year, as well as **"Storytelling Saturdays"** with professional storytellers for children 5 through 12. These are generally held on the second Saturday of each month. For further information, call 619-696-1966. **(Note** that admission for Storytelling Saturdays is $5.00 for children, free for accompanying adults. Reservations are recommended for these events.)

Other Attractions

☆ Centro Cultural de la Raza

> 619-235-6135; 2125 Park Boulevard. Open Thursday-Sunday noon to 5:00 P.M. Admission: free.

The art and culture of Mexicans, Chicanos, and Native Americans are preserved and promoted in this creative center. Whether you claim your heritage from one of those three groups, or whether you simply have a healthy appreciation for the richness of San Diego's culture, the ever-changing art gallery and performances offered in the Centro are well worth a visit. Kids of any cultural background can learn to dance the lively *Ballet Folklórico* of Mexico through lessons offered here. (See Chapter 8, "Adventures of the Mind.)

☆ WorldBeat Center

> 619-230-1190 or www.worldbeatcenter.org; 2100 Park Boulevard (at Pepper Grove). Admission: Free.

African and African-American cultures are featured here through art, music, and dance. Kids can sign up for classes in African dance and in African drum making. Watch this center also for music festivals, particularly reggae.

☆ House of Pacific Relations

619-234-0739; Pan American Rd. West. Open Sundays, noon to 5:00 P.M. Admission: free.

This group of small cottages, each home to a different nation, holds open house on Sunday afternoons. In all, twenty-eight different ethnic groups from around the world are represented. Between March and October, the lawn between the cottages becomes the scene of a festival at 2:00 each Sunday, with ethnic food, traditional costumes, music, folk dancing, and crafts.

☆ Morley Field Sports Complex

619-692-4919

Located in the northeast corner of Balboa Park, this area offers nature trails in Florida Canyon for hiking or mountain biking, an archery range (bring your own equipment), a velodrome for bicycle enthusiasts, and a disk golf course. All-day use fee for the **Frisbee golf** course is $1 on weekdays, $1.50 on weekends. Children under 7 can play free. You can even rent a Frisbee for $1.50/day if you haven't brought your own.

The trails in Florida Canyon make for great games of hide-and-seek!

☆ Spanish Village Art Center

619-233-9050; 1770 Village Place. Open 11:00 to 4:00 daily.

Spanish Village, located near the entrance to the Zoo, is a charming area of old Spanish-style cottages around a small "plaza." Local artists and craftsmen rent space here and welcome the onlookers who cluster around them. Children enjoy the immediacy of the experience, and can watch a work of art

Spanish Village

actually taking shape before their eyes. Of course, the artisans are happy to sell their wares to interested shoppers.

☆ United Nations Gift Shop

619-233-5044; at the United Nations Building. Open daily.

Located near the international cottages, this shop carries cards and gifts.

MISCELLANEOUS

On Sundays at 2:00 there are free organ concerts at the Spreckels Organ Pavilion. Street performers (mimes, jugglers, magicians, etc.) abound in the park Sunday afternoons. The lily pond, near the botanical garden, is a wonderful spot for whiling away a dreamy half-hour or so; kids enjoy watching the fish that live in its waters, and the lily pads are beautiful.

When you plan an adventure with kids in Balboa Park, you might consider bringing a picnic lunch. There are several restaurants and snack bars available (the café in the Art Museum's sculpture garden and the snack bar in the Ruben Fleet Space Center are both reasonably kid-friendly.) But there are so many lovely picnic spots among the trees and gardens, pools and fountains; a picnic is probably the best family dining available.

CHAPTER 3

Beach and Bay Adventures

BEACHES

San Diego's beaches are what folks imagine when they dream of southern California: surf and sand and palm trees under a friendly sun. The best time to enjoy the beach is in September, after the crowds of tourists have left. The days are warmer than ever, and the ocean temperature is often at its best. The dreariest month of the year at San Diego beaches is usually June, when low clouds can often obscure the sun for days on end. But even summer visitors, or residents enjoying leisure time in the summer months, can find relatively uncrowded beaches with a little persistence.

No ground fires are permitted on any San Diego beaches. Glass containers are prohibited on all beaches, and a few beaches prohibit alcoholic beverages. Not all beaches have life-

Fun on the water is a favorite activity in San Diego.

Be sure to bring shoes (the sand can be hot) and plenty of sun- screen, as well as a container of drinking water. Many families also bring a beach umbrella or other man-made shade, as beaches offer little natural shade. If you plan to stay for a sunset barbecue, bring warm clothing, as the tem- perature often drops rapidly along with the set- ting sun.

guards during the off season; check, if this is important to you, by calling one of the phone numbers provided below. Because beach conditions vary from year to year, it is a good idea to call ahead anyway. (For example, a beach that has plenty of sand this year could be nothing but rock next year, depending on what the winter storms have done. Also, unfortunately, now and then a beach may close temporarily due to accidents such as sewage spills or other contaminating events.)

During the summer, most San Diego communities pro- vide **special buses** to and from the beach areas. Some of these buses also carry bike racks. For details, call your local transit district.

The beaches listed below are those most suitable to chil- dren, with relatively easy access. Beaches are listed from north to south.

Oceanside

(760-435-4018)

☆ Tyson Street Park

Directions: From I-5 take the Mission Ave. exit and head west. Turn right on Hill St. In one block, turn left on 3rd St. Turn left on Pacific St. and look for the playground and small parking lot. This lot fills up early, so you may have to find street parking.

This is a wide, sandy beach with lifeguards, **a playground**, sev- eral choices for food service, and restrooms. Swimming areas and surfing areas are kept separate, which is a good safety fea- ture. **Oceanside Pier** is just to the north of the playground area.

☆ Buccaneer Beach

Directions: From I-5 take the Oceanside Boulevard exit and head west. Turn left on Pacific Street and look for the park- ing lot and grassy park.

This beach features restrooms, showers, a snack bar, and a lifeguard station. An extra attraction is the little adjoining **grassy park with picnic tables, barbecues, and shade.**

Carlsbad

☆ Carlsbad Beach

Directions: From I-5 take the Tamarack exit and head west. Continue to Carlsbad Boulevard and turn left. Look for the parking lot.

This stretch of beach, for about a mile and a half north, includes a few **fire rings** for barbecues, as well as restrooms, showers, and several lifeguard stands.

☆ South Carlsbad State Beach

(760-438-3143). From I-5 take the La Costa exit and head west to Carlsbad Boulevard (Old 101); turn north and access from Ponto Drive.

This is another long stretch of beach with **fire rings** and facilities. Some claim that the water is especially warm just off the power plant!

Encinitas

☆ Moonlight Beach

(760-944-3398; or 760-633-2880 for recorded information.) Directions: Take the Encinitas Boulevard exit off I-5 and head west. There are parking lots on C Street and on 3ʳᵈ Street.

Moonlight Beach is a favorite with the **beach volleyball** crowd. **Fire rings**, picnic tables, **snack bar**, restrooms and shower, and a lifeguard stand all make this a favorite family beach.

Cardiff

☆ Cardiff State Beach

(760-753-5091) Directions: From I-5 take the Lomas Santa Fe exit and go west to 1ˢᵗ Street (Old 101); turn north.

Check the phone number to see whether there is adequate sand on Cardiff State Beach for a family outing, since in recent years the sand here has tended to come and go with the seasons.

This is a lovely beach with a parking lot, fewer crowds, and wonderful **tide pools** (see section on Tide Pools below.) There are restrooms, showers, and a lifeguard tower.

Solana Beach

☆ Solana Beach County Park

(858-755-1569 for marine safety; or 858-755-2971 for recorded weather and surf information.) Directions: From I-5 take the Lomas Santa Fe exit and go directly to the end.

A favorite surf spot, this beach is also less crowded than many. (The local surfers call it "Pill Box" for the concrete retaining walls.) There are rest rooms, showers, and **fire rings**. **Exceptionally easy access.**

Del Mar

(General beach information: 858-755-1556).

☆ Dog Beach

Directions: From I-5 take the Via de la Valle exit and go west to Camino del Mar (Old 101). Turn left and look for street parking just north of the mouth of the San Dieguito River, where the beach area forms a little estuary. Bring quarters, as the parking is metered. Or you can pay $4.00 for the all-day parking lot.

There are **no facilities** here, but the family dog will be able to join you, and the shallow estuary makes a nice spot for the small fry to splash and play safely. During the summer months, dogs must be leashed. From October to May, they are allowed to run free. You are, of course, expected to clean up after your pooch!

☆ Seagrove Park

Directions: From I-5 take the Del Mar Heights exit and head north on Camino del Mar. Turn left on 15th Street.

If you go to Dog Beach, remember that, although most dogs are friendly, some may reflexively snap or snarl at an unwitting youngster. Also remember to watch where you step! Owners are asked to clean up after their canine companions, but that's not always so easy to do.

Kid and dogs frolicking at Dog Beach.

There are **fire rings** at the north end of this beach. The **grassy park** is a wonderful place to toss a frisbee or to picnic, and there is a children's playground. There are **no facilities** on this beach, but there are many restaurants in the area.

La Jolla

☆ Torrey Pines State Beach

> **(858-755-2063)** Take I-5 to Carmel Valley Road. Turn left onto McGonigle Road to the parking lot, where you will find restrooms and fairly easy beach access. Note that there is a $4.00 fee for parking here. This fee covers the cost of entering the preserve. There is also sometimes free roadside parking on the western side of North Torrey Pines Road (the coast highway, southern continuation of Camino del Mar or Old Highway 101.)

Torrey Pines State Beach is justifiably one of the most popular beaches in the county. It includes showers and a lifeguard tower. **Picnic tables, fire rings,** and the **hiking trail** that leads up to beautiful Torrey Pines State Park make this beach an all-day adventure. The waters off this beach are a **marine pre-**

31

serve, making them especially attractive for exploring with a snorkel and mask.

☆ La Jolla Shores

Directions: From I-5, take the La Jolla Village Drive exit. At Torrey Pines Rd., go north, then turn left on La Jolla Shores Drive. You will pass Scripps Institute of Oceanography; take a right on Calle del Collado and a left on Paseo Grande. Look for the parking lot near grassy Kellogg Park.

I avoid La Jolla Shores and La Jolla Cove in the summer because of the difficulty finding parking. If you're determined to go, go early in the day!

The easy surf entry and long wide beach make this a favorite with scuba diving classes; groups of "frogmen" can be seen in all seasons waddling down to the water's edge. The crowds here in summer are huge, and the parking lot is eternally full. Other parking is at a premium. **Fire rings**, restrooms, lifeguards, **a playground,** and the **adjacent grassy park** with its picnic tables and shade, all add to the attraction of "The Shores."

☆ La Jolla Cove

Directions: From the north, take I-5 to La Jolla Village Drive and turn west. At Torrey Pines Road, turn left. Continue 2.75 miles to Prospect Street and turn right. Look for Coast Boulevard, and follow it downhill toward the ocean. From the south, exit I-5 on Ardath Road. It will merge with Torrey Pines Road. From there, follow the above directions. Be advised that parking is at a premium during summer months.

"The Cove" is a small secluded beach that is a great favorite with snorkelers and scuba divers, as it is a marine preserve. With **mask** and **snorkel**, you can see brilliant garibaldi fish and the unique kelp forests of this area. California sea lions sometimes sun themselves on the rocks off the beach. At the north end of the cove are some small but rewarding **tide pools**. Parking isn't easy, and the beach can be crowded here. But if your youngster is a budding marine biologist or sport diver, it's well worth the effort! Restrooms and showers are available.

☆ Ellen Scripps Park

Just south of The Cove (see above.)

This **grassy beach-side park** offers picnic tables, barbecues, restrooms, snacks, and lifeguards. Like all the La Jolla beaches, it is very popular and crowded during tourist season.

Pacific Beach

(Information about Pacific Beach beaches is best obtained through the Pacific Beach Department of Parks and Recreation at 858-581-9927).

☆ North Pacific Beach

Directions: From I-5 take the Garnet Ave. exit. Turn west on Garnet; when it forms a "Y", take the right-hand branch. At Mission Boulevard, turn right and go three blocks to Diamond St. Turn left and look for the small beach parking lot.

North Pacific Beach has restrooms, **fire rings**, and lifeguards. A short walk south along the beach brings you to **Crystal Pier**, and there are lots of restaurants on the streets by the pier.

☆ South Pacific Beach

Directions: Follow the directions for North Pacific Beach above, but turn left onto Mission Boulevard instead of right. South Pacific Beach can be accessed by any east-west street.

There are restrooms, **fire rings**, life guards, and snack services here, and lots of sand. This is a favorite **surfing spot**, especially close to the pier, so watch out for your little ones.

Mission Beach

Directions: Access all along the southern end of Mission Boulevard (see Pacific Beach directions above.) Or, take I-8 to the Sports Arena Blvd. exit, turn right from the off-ramp and follow the signs onto West Mission Bay Drive. Follow West Mission Bay Drive to Mission Bay Boulevard. Turn either left or right onto Mission Bay Boulevard—there's beach everywhere!

This is probably the longest unbroken stretch of beach in the county. You will find everything here: **fire rings**, full rest rooms, and a long chain of lifeguard stands, as well as some of southern California's most colorful characters. The **Mission Beach Promenade**, paralleling the beach, is a southern California playland for kids of all ages who roll along on bicycles, skateboards, and roller skates. You can watch the show, or you can rent roller skates or bikes and join the crowd!

Ocean Beach

☆ Dog Beach

See tip for Dog Beach in Del Mar. above.

Directions: Take I-8 west to the end of the freeway, turn left, and follow signs to Sunset Cliffs Boulevard. Turn right on West Point Loma Boulevard and right again at Voltaire.

Like Dog Beach in Del Mar, this beach offers as its main attraction a playground for the family dog, along with the kids. Not only can Fido run free here 365 days a year, but he/she will almost always find lots of canine companionship. For Fido's human companions, there are **fire rings**, rest rooms, and lifeguards.

☆ Ocean Beach Park

Directions: Follow the directions above for Dog Beach, but follow Sunset Cliffs Boulevard past Voltaire and turn right on Brighton or any of the subsequent five or six streets. They all lead to the beach.

If you have small fry. keep them out of the way of incoming boards!

There are plenty of **fire rings**, restrooms, and lifeguards, and there are many food services on the streets just off the beach. At the southern end of Ocean Beach Park is the **Ocean Beach fishing pier**. The closer you are to the pier, the better the surfing gets! If you have a budding surfer in your family, he or she can mingle here with San Diego's finest.

Coronado

☆ Coronado City Beach

Directions: From the Coronado Bridge, turn left on Orange Ave. and follow the signs to Ocean Boulevard. Turn right on Ocean Boulevard.

There are restrooms, showers, **fire rings**, and a guard tower here. This municipal beach is less well known, and therefore **less crowded**, than other near-by beaches.

☆ Silver Strand State Beach

(619-435-5184). Directions: From I-5 take the Palm Ave. exit in Imperial Beach (Note: There is also a Palm Ave. exit in Chula Vista! It's easy to confuse them if you're unfamiliar with South County.) Follow Palm Ave. west, and then veer right onto Silver Strand Boulevard. Watch for the sign that says "Silver Strand State Park" and turn in there.

This is a very wide sandy beach, with plenty of parking, restrooms, **fire rings**, **picnic tables**, and lifeguards. **Note:** There is a $4.00 fee for parking, as it is a state park.

Imperial Beach

Directions: From I-5 take the Palm Ave. exit in Imperial Beach, and go west to Seacoast Drive. Turn left and access the beach at any point.

This beach is a favorite of locals for its **fishing pier** (see section on Piers below) and for its **picnic facilities.** In July, it gains county-wide attention as the site of the annual sand castle competition. Each year the sand castles grow more elaborate and more beautiful, until the sea claims them for another season. This event is a great treat for families (see Appendix 1). At the

Exploring tide pools at La Jolla Cove

Palm Avenue (north) end of the beach there is a lifeguard tower, showers, and restrooms.

TIDE POOLS

A small rock pool by the edge of the sea contains a whole world where crabs scuttle and fish play and marine gardens flourish. Sharing these discoveries with your youngster makes for a special adventure for both of you. The best time to go tidepooling is when the tide is receding.

Wear old rubber-soled shoes that you don't mind getting wet, and watch out for slippery patches on wet rocks!

Tide tables can be obtained at most surf shops and/or dive shops. Many newspapers publish the tide schedules for the day; and the city and county lifeguard stations always have that information available. Be sure to leave the tide pool just as you found it for the benefit of the marine creatures that live there and the human creatures who will come to enjoy it after you.

Note that the Birch Aquarium sponsors tide pool outings for families. For more information, call them at 858-534-7336.

The following is a partial listing of the best tide pool areas in San Diego. Tide pools are listed from north to south:

☆ Swami's Beach

From I-5, take the Encinitas Boulevard exit. Go west to 1st St. (old Highway 101) and head south to just beyond K St. where you will see the domes of the Self Realization Fellowship. You can park in the lot by Sea Cliff Park.

☆ Cardiff State Beach

See directions above for access to Cardiff State Beach.

There are wonderful and **easily accessible** tide pools at the south end of this beach. Tidepooling here can be combined with an afternoon of swimming and sunning.

Access to Swami's is via a long, steep wooden staircase that may be difficult for very young children.

☆ Tide Beach Park

From I-5, take the Lomas Santa Fe exit to Highway 101. Turn right and look for Solana Vista Drive. Turn left and follow to Pacific Ave.

Access is moderately difficult, and not recommended for small children.

The large reef and the many tide pools here make it a great beach for serious tidepoolers.

☆ Scripps Beach

Take La Jolla Shores Drive off of Torrey Pines Road. Park near Scripps Institute of Oceanography, and look for the tide pools just north of the pier.

☆ Bird Rock—San Diego (southern end of La Jolla)

From La Jolla Boulevard, go west on Bird Rock Ave. to the end of the street.

Scripps and Bird Rock have no facilities, but for an hour's tidepooling, the rocks are wonderful.

☆ Mission Beach Jetty

> See directions above for access to Mission Beach. The jetty is at the south end of Mission Beach.

You can combine a day at the beach or on the Mission Beach Promenade with a tide pool adventure.

☆ Point Loma Tide Pools

> Take I-8 West until it ends. Turn left on Nimitz. From Nimitz, turn right onto Rosecrans. From Rosecrans, turn right onto Highway 209 and proceed through the Navy base toward the Cabrillo National Monument. Just before the information kiosk for the Cabrillo National Monument, Cabrillo Road branches off to the right. Follow that road down to the small parking lot by the tidepool area.

These are probably the best tide pools in the San Diego area, especially during autumn and winter. The **Cabrillo National Monument** is described in Chapter 7, "Adventures in Time"; an excursion here in January or February could include whale watching as well as tidepooling.

BAY ADVENTURES

A day at the bay is a way to enjoy the beach without the surf. With babies or very young children, this is sometimes a great option!

San Diego is blessed not only with some of the most beautiful beaches in the country, but also with two splendid bays ringed with their own fine beaches and recreational areas. Mission Bay and San Diego Bay have little or no surf, so they have become centers for water sports and for those who prefer their salt water calm and smooth.

Mission Bay (San Diego)

On summer weekend afternoons, Mission Bay looks like a giant playground for children of all ages. Is your family active? Bring your **bicycles** (or rent them in Mission Bay Park at various locations) and ride the pleasant, flat trails for miles around the bay. Are you toting small children? Park yourselves near one of the **playgrounds** where tots can alternate between swings and the calm swimming waters off the bay's beach.

Hungry? Many areas provide **picnic tables**, and Fiesta Island has **fire rings**. Barbecues in your own containers are permitted everywhere. (Of course, ground fires are prohibited.) Fishermen all have their favorite spots, both off the shore and from boats. There are several public ramps for boat launching, and there are special areas designated for water-skiers to keep them away from the fish.

☆ Mission Bay Visitor Center

(619-276-8200). **Directions: From I-5, take the Clairemont Drive west to East Mission Bay Drive. Drive across East Mission Bay Drive directly into the parking lot.**

If you are a first time visitor to Mission Bay, or an old timer who needs new information, stop here first. You will find maps, brochures, and a friendly staff to orient you. You will also find delightful walking, jogging, skating, and biking along the concrete walkways, a sandy beach, a grassy area that includes a playground and tot-lot, restrooms, and barbecue areas with tables.

☆ Family Areas

A number of areas around the bay offer lifeguard service during the summer months, playgrounds for both tiny tots and older children, restrooms with showers and changing areas, and picnic tables, as well as convenient parking. A few are listed below, but your family may discover its own favorite spot.

- **Mission Bay Park** is located just beyond the Visitor Center (See directions above.) It offers picnic tables, playgrounds, and concrete walkways for skating, jogging, or strolling. **Good for baby strollers!**

- **Bonita Cove,** between Mission Beach and Mariner's Point. From I-8 take the Sports Arena/Ingraham exit. Take Ingraham across the San Diego River floodway, and watch for the signs to West Mission Bay Drive. Take West Mission Bay Drive across the channel and into Mission Bay Park. Watch for signs to Bonita Cove.

- **De Anza Cove**, at the north end of Mission Bay Drive. Follow above directions to Mission Bay Visitor Center, but turn right on East Mission Bay Drive and continue to Mission Bay Park/De Anza Cove.

- **Fiesta Island**, just across the channel from Sea World. From I-5, take the Sea World Drive exit. Just after exiting, turn right on Fiesta Island Rd. and follow it onto the island. **Note** that **dogs** are allowed off-leash on Fiesta Island.

- **Leisure Lagoon**, just north of the Hilton Hotel. Follow above directions to Mission Bay Visitors Center, but turn left on East Mission Bay Drive and watch for signs just before the Hilton Hotel.

- **Santa Clara Point**, north of Bahia Point. Follow the above directions for Bonita Cove, but stay on West Mission Bay Drive to Mission Boulevard. Turn right and follow Mission Boulevard to Santa Clara Place. Turn right.

- **Mission Point**, just opposite Mariners Point. Follow the above directions for Santa Clara Point, but instead of turning right on Mission Boulevard, turn left. Follow Mission Boulevard to its end.

San Diego Bay (San Diego and South County)

The beaches and parks along San Diego Bay tend to be a little less crowded during "high season" than those of Mission Bay. Both **Shelter Island** and **Harbor Island** have small sand beaches, parking lots, grass, shade, restrooms, and picnic tables. Shelter Island is reached by taking the Rosecrans exit from I-5 or from I-8, and following Rosecrans to Shelter Island Drive. The beach area is on the eastern side of the island. Harbor Island is reached by following the signs to the Lindbergh Field airport from I-5. As you approach the airport on Harbor Drive, watch for an exit to Harbor Island. The beach isn't on Harbor Island—it is in the area known as Spanish Landing Park, located across from the north end of the island.

Bayside Park in Chula Vista is a favorite with locals from the South County area. To get there, take the J Street exit off

Pier fishing is a popular pastime

of I-5 in Chula Vista, and turn right on Marina Parkway. There are restrooms, showers, grass, shade, parking lots, and lovely sand beaches.

Tidelands Park in Coronado is the green stretch that you see below you as you cross the bridge onto the island of Coronado. There's a sandy beach, a playground, picnic tables, and restrooms. To get there, turn right when you come off the bridge; then make another right on Glorietta and a right on Mullinix Drive.

The beach at the **Ferry Landing** in Coronado is small, but delightful, especially for families with young children. There are no waves, the water is warm, and there are restaurants, snack bars, and restrooms within easy access. The trolley or the train takes you close to the Broadway Pier, where you can catch a ferry to Coronado and virtually step right onto the beach, making possible a delightful family outing with no parking hassles!

PIERS

"Gone Fishin'" is the sign every fisherman wants to post at the door to his home or office, and kids love to share this pastime. Dropping a line off of a pier is free, and in most cases no fishing license is required. Most of the piers are easily accessible by public transportation, making this a no-hassle adventure for families. Below are listed a few of the family-friendly piers in the county.

☆ Shelter Island Pier

(619-222-7635). Directions: From I-5 take the Rosecrans exit; take Rosecrans south to Shelter Island Drive.

Bait shop and snack bar. Open 24 hours.

☆ Crystal Pier

(858-483-6983). Directions: From I-5 take Garnet west to the end.

Open 7:00 A.M. to sundown.

A young friend of mine says that one of his happiest childhood memories is going pier fishing with his dad at midnight.

No fishing license required for children under 16; **for adults, license is required.** Cost for one year's license is $13.25. **Note:** Bait and tackle can be purchased at Crystal Pier, but the fishing license cannot. The various fishing boat landings on nearby Shelter Island sell fishing licenses.

☆ Ocean Beach Pier

(619-226-3474). Directions: Take I-8 west to the end. Turn left and follow to Sunset Cliffs Blvd. Turn left on Niagara off of Sunset Cliffs.

Bait shop. Open 24 hours.

They would bring a lantern and a radio, and enjoy the special bonding of being together in the middle of the night. After a breakfast of fresh fried fish, they'd sleep the morning away.

☆ Imperial Beach Pier

(619-423-8328). From I-5 take the Palm Ave. exit west to Seacoast Drive; go south on Seacoast for about 6 blocks.

No bait shop on the pier, but bait available in the market at the foot of the pier. Open 24 hours.

☆ Oceanside Pier

(760-435-4018). Directions: From I-5 take the Mission Avenue exit. Follow Mission west to Pacific Street and turn right.

Bait shop and restaurant. **Open** 24 hours.

The Ocean Beach Pier

SPECIAL MARINE ADVENTURES

☆ Grunion Runs

On certain special nights, some of San Diego's beaches come alive with thousands of shimmering creatures. The grunion fish come ashore in droves to spawn, and then disappear again into their ocean homes. To find out when the grunion runs are predicted, call your local lifeguard station (see phone numbers under the "Beaches" section above) or Scripps Aquarium (858-534-3474). As a general rule, grunion appear on the second, third, and fourth nights after the highest monthly tide between March and September. The sandy beaches of Mission Beach and Pacific Beach are particularly good spots for grunion hunting.

Children under 16 may collect grunion between March and August without a California fishing license. (For adults, a license is required.) In June, a "Grunion Festival" is held on the beach south of Crystal Pier in Pacific Beach. It features grunion, but includes Native American singers and dancers, as well as exhibits.

Marine creatures, like humans, don't always behave in a predictable fashion. If you go on a grunion hunt, be prepared; the fish may not arrive on cue! Bring other entertainment (marshmallows to roast, stories to tell) in case the grunion don't show.

☆ La Jolla Caves

La Jolla Cave Shop, 1325 Cave Street in La Jolla, at the corner of Coast Boulevard. (858-459-0746)

Open 9-5 daily. During the summer, the shop is open until 8:00 P.M. daily. Admission: Adults $2, Children 3 years to 11 years, $1.

Centuries of wind and tides and waves have carved the cliffs of La Jolla into a series of natural caves, most of which are accessible only by boat. But one of them, known as Sunny Jim Cave, is accessible by a hundred-year-old staircase carved into the sandstone during the first years of the twentieth century. Just the descent itself, down 133 stairs into a dimly-lit and winding tunnel, is an adventure for

Forget baby strollers here! If your kids can't walk the long staircase themselves, come back when they're older.

kids—their imaginations will take off. A wooden platform at the bottom allows you to stand inside the cave without getting wet while you discover crabs creeping along the rocks, birds nesting in the cave's recesses, and the occasional golden garibaldi fish.

☆ Children's Pool/Seal Rock Marine Mammal Preserve

Coast Boulevard in La Jolla, just south of La Jolla Cove (see "Beaches" section above).

Locals still refer to this little La Jolla beach as "The Children's Pool." Since the water is calm and relatively shallow here, it was a long-time favorite of families with small children. However, a few years ago a colony of California harbor seals decided that those very conditions were just what they had been seeking for their home, and they moved in. For those with an open spirit (and children almost always are open-spirited), this turn of events simply means another adventure. There is a walk-

You might want to bring a pair of binoculars and a picnic to enjoy in the nearby grassy park.

way from which it is easy to view the seals, and it's worth a visit to watch them sunning, swimming, and interacting with one another in a setting that is their true habitat. In February and March, the new pups are "on display."

☆ Leopard Sharks

In September, schools of leopard sharks appear in the shallow waters just off the beach at La Jolla Shores. (See "Beaches" section above.) With just a simple face mask and snorkel—or even just a face mask—kids can get up close and personal with these awesome but harmless creatures of the deep. For the predicted dates of their appearance, call the Stephen Birch Aquarium at 858-534-3474.

☆ La Jolla Visitor Center

7966 Herschel Avenue (near Prospect Street).

Open 10-5, Thursday through Tuesday during the Winter; 10-7 every day during the Summer. (619-236-1212)

The La Jolla Visitors Center is a walk-in center only. For more information, visit www.sandiego.org or www.lajollabythesea.com.

☆ Whale Watching

Between mid-December and mid-February every year, the ocean waters of San Diego become the site of a marvelous parade as the California gray whales migrate some 6,000 miles from Alaska to the Baja California lagoons where they give birth to their calves. On their way, they cruise through our own local waters, and whale watchers can see them spout and breach, and sometimes even play or feed near shore. During March, they head back north along the same invisible ocean lanes.

For "land-lubbers," a great spot for whale watching during this season is the lighthouse at the Cabrillo National Monument (see Chapter 7, "Adventures in Time"). Each January, Cabrillo National Monument sponsors a Whale Watch Weekend, featuring films and live presentations. Call 619-557-5450 for more information.

Remember to dress warmly and bring binoculars. Consult your physician for medications against motion sickness if this is a problem for you.

For those prepared to take to the seas in pursuit of these magnificent mammals, there are a number of whale-watching cruises available.

- **Birch Aquarium**—During whale-watching season, Birch Aquarium offers more than thirty different opportunities to cruise with a naturalist from Scripps Institute. These whale-watching cruises are open to children from age 5 on up (with an adult.) Each trip lasts for 2 ½ hours. Prices are $12 for children ages 5-15 and $17 for adults (16 and up.) To register, call Seaforth Sportfishing at 619-224-7767 and request the Aquarium Cruise. Seaforth Sportfishing also runs SeaWorld's whale watching cruises during the winter season.

- **San Diego Harbor Excursion** (619-234-4111); 1050 N. Harbor Drive, San Diego; Adults, $19.50; Seniors $17.50; Children 4-12, $9.75.

- **Hornblower Cruises** (619-686-8715); 1066 N. Harbor Drive, San Diego; Adults, $21.50; Children 4-12, $10.75.

These boats generally take folks around San Diego Harbor for sightseeing tours, so they are a little more comfortably appointed than the commercial fishing boats described below. During the winter months, whale-watching cruises are added to the usual harbor excursions.

☆ Commercial Fishing Boats

The ocean fishing boats listed below offer whale watching cruises during "Whale Season." They are usually out for 2 or 3 hours. Their crews are friendly, helpful, and very knowledgeable. Prices range from $15 to $20 for adults, with discounts for children and seniors. Call for exact updated prices.

- **Helgren's** (760-722-2133); 315 Harbor Drive South, Oceanside. (North County Coastal)

- **Islandia Sport Fishing** (619-222-1164); 1551 W. Mission Bay Drive, San Diego.

- **Seaforth Sportfishing** (619-224-3383); 1717 Quivera Rd. San Diego.

- **Point Loma Sportsfishing** (619-223-1627); 1403 Scott St. San Diego.

- **Red Rooster III** (619-224-3857); 2801 Emerson St. San Diego.

BEACH AND BAY CAMPING

There are four state beaches in San Diego County where camping is permitted: **San Onofre State Beach** (North County Coastal) at 949-492-4872, **South Carlsbad State Beach** (North County Coastal) at 760-438-3143, **San Elijo State Beach** (North County Coastal) at 760-753-5091, and **Silver Strand State Beach** (South County) at 619-435-5184. All of these are popular with locals as well as with tourists, and reservations go fast; to obtain a site during the summer months, you should call in January. There is plenty of information available about all of California's state parks on their website at at http://cal-parks.ca.gov. To make a camping reservation, call 1-800-444-PARK or go through the website of an organization called Reserve America at www. reserveamerica.com. The state parks' basic fee structure is $8 to $12 per vehicle per night for developed sites, with $6 more for use of hook-ups to water and/or electricity. For detailed information on these and other public campgrounds in San Diego County, consult Jeff Tyler's *Campgrounds of San Diego County.*

When choosing a spot for beach camping, consider the ease of access to the beach. Parents are usually the ones hauling beach chairs, umbrellas, towels, food, and small people up and down the stairs, possibly several times a day.

In addition to camping on a state beach, families can camp on Mission Bay at one of several private campgrounds. They are more expensive than state beaches, but less expensive than taking the family to a hotel or motel—and probably a lot more fun! **Campland on the Bay** (800-4-BAY-FUN) offers a private beach, boat rentals and a boat launch facility, playgrounds and organized activities for children, and two heated pools. **De Anza Harbor Resort** (800-924-PLAY) has paved campsites only, so is not appropriate for tent camping. However, they do offer a recreation room, children's play-

Most of the campgrounds that include swimming pools do not have lifeguard service. If your children are not 100% water safe, you might want to request a campsite far away from the pool.

ground, and private beach as well as windsurfing and sailing. Fees for both campgrounds vary with the season and with what kind of hook-ups you choose; during the summer, you will pay between $22 and $50 per night for four people; after Labor Day, fees drop to around $18.50 to $35 per night.

CHAPTER 4

Adventures in Parks and Lakes

An adventure in one of San Diego's parks can be an all-day affair, beginning with the special thrill of rising before dawn to be at the lake by daybreak when the fish are hungriest and ending with a barbecue under the trees at dusk. Or it can be as simple as an hour's break in the middle of the day to visit the swings at a neighborhood park. In any case, it is almost always a refreshing change of scene and change of pace, and is adaptable to all ages and all interests.

Every community has its **local park or parks**, and it is beyond the scope of this book to detail every park in San Diego County. The Pacific Bell Yellow Pages telephone directory has a listing in the front (the blue-rimmed pages) of community parks, and the Pacific Bell White Pages telephone directory has

One of San Diego's many neighborhood parks

a listing for each town's Department of Parks and Recreation. Look for your community in the blue pages under "City Government" listings. Additionally, the *Thomas Guide: San Diego County* has a very complete listing of neighborhood parks in the back section under "Parks and Recreation."

COUNTY PARKS

The County of San Diego maintains a number of open-space areas throughout the county that offer enjoyment to families. Some county parks are in or near major communities and function like neighborhood parks, offering accessible islands of nature within our urbanized world. A few of these "local" county parks are described below, along with those suitable for camping.

You can count on finding rest rooms in all of the county parks. This can make or break an outing with little ones!

For general information on county parks, call 858-694-3049 or see the website, www.co.san-diego.ca.us/parks. To reserve a campsite at any of the county parks described below, you must call the County Parks office at 858-565-3600, or stop by their office at 5201 Ruffin Road, Ste. P, San Diego, 92123. Basic fees run from approximately $18 per night for full hook-up (water, electricity, sewer) to an average of $16 per night for partial hook-up (water and electricity) to approximately $14 per night for no hook-up. There is also a $3.00 reservation fee.

Note that for most of the parks listed below, there is a day-use fee of $2 per vehicle.

☆ Sweetwater County Park (South County)

From I-805, exit in Chula Vista on Bonita Road (State Route 17) and head northeast to San Miguel Road. Bear right, and follow San Miguel Road to Summit Meadow Road. Take a left on Summit Meadow to the park entrance.

The Sweetwater River winds through this lovely park. There are picnic areas and wide, grassy fields, as well as trails for mountain biking, horseback riding, jogging, or just strolling. **Family campsites** are available by the Sweetwater Reservoir, and an **equestrian campground** is also available for families exploring the county on horseback.

☆ Flinn Springs Park (East County)

Take I-8 just past Lakeside and exit on Old Highway 80. Turn into the park at Marina Springs Lane.

The Los Coches Creek runs through this little park, on its way to the San Diego River. You'll find lots of shade from the fine old oak trees, along with picnic tables, ball fields, and hiking trails. Kids can sometimes spot tadpoles in the creek during the spring months.

☆ Louis A. Stelzer Park (East County)

From Highway 67 in Lakeside, exit on Mapleview St. and go east to to Ashwood St.. Turn left on Ashwood St. and go north till it becomes Wildcat Canyon Rd. Continue north and it will lead you right into Louis A. Stelzer Park.

The unique feature of this park is that its designers were particularly attuned to the needs of those who use wheelchairs. The **wheelchair exercise course** is an experience that all kids will enjoy! In addition, there are picnic tables and hiking trails for everyone's use. Primitive **camping** facilities are available here for youth groups who want to make it a weekend outing.

☆ Felicita Park (North County Inland)

From I-15, take the Via Rancho Parkway exit and head west. Turn right on Felicita Rd. and then left on Clarence Lane into the park.

A little stream runs through this charming park—at least during wet years. In addition, Felicita Park offers horseshoe and volleyball courts, a ball field, playgrounds and tot lots, and picnic tables, as well as a museum and a stage.

☆ Dos Picos County Park (North County Inland)

Take State Highway 67 toward Ramona, make a sharp right on Mussey Grade Rd. and then right again on Dos Picos Park Rd. into the park.

This pleasant, family-oriented park includes horseshoe courts, a playground and tot lot, picnic tables, hiking trails, and a small lake. If you keep your eyes open, you can find Native American grinding stones dating back thousands of years, once used to grind acorns from the great-grandparents of the oak trees that grace the park today. Fine **campsites** are available.

☆ William Heise County Park (North County Inland)

Located near Julian. From Santa Ysabel, go east 6 miles on Highway 78 to Pine Hills Road. Turn right and proceed south 2.2 miles to Frisius Road. Turn left; the campground is about 2.5 miles ahead. Bear right at Heise Park Road to park entrance.

Oak, pine, and cedar grace this lovely back country park. There are beautiful trails to hike, including some that offer views of both desert and sea on clear days. Rangers lead nature hikes and provide evening campfire programs. **Campsites** are available, as are **cabins** sleeping 4 to 6 people.

☆ Live Oak Park (North County Inland)

Take I-15 toward Fallbrook and exit on Mission Rd/Old Hwy 395. Go south on Old Highway 395 to Reche Rd (State Route 15.) Turn right and follow Reche Rd. to its intersection with Gird Rd. where you will find the park entrance.

This is one of the county's prettiest parks, with two streams winding through shady groves of oak. You will find a fenced play area, several ball fields and picnic areas, and two miles of easy hiking trails. Our county's original inhabitants enjoyed this special spot; you should be able to find their grinding stones here and there under the oak trees.

☆ Guajome Regional Park (North County Coastal)

From State Highway 76, exit on North Santa Fe Ave. and follow it southeast to Guajome Lake Rd. where you will turn south into the park.

This is a great park for spotting birds and butterflies. **Fishing** is permitted in the little lake (fishing license required), and there are playgrounds, picnic areas, and hiking trails, as well as equestrian trails. A restored historic adobe, Rancho Guajome Adobe, is part of the park. Tours are given each weekend at 11:00, 12:30, and 2:00.

☆ San Dieguito County Park (North County Coastal)

From I-5 take the Lomas Santa Fe exit in Solana Beach and head east. Turn left on Highland and watch for the park entrance in 0.25 miles.

Close to the ocean, San Dieguito County Park is often cooler in the summer than are some of the more inland parks. There are nature trails to explore, swinging bridges and lookout towers to stimulate the imagination of young explorers, a pond where you can watch the local waterfowl, and a shallow stream that's just right for toddlers to wade in. There are picnic tables, barbecues, ball fields, and play areas.

LAKES

The city of San Diego includes almost thirty lakes, most of them man-made and stocked with fish for anglers of all ages. Many other cities in the area boast their own lakes, and the county of San Diego includes several lovely lakes in park-like settings. Generations of San Diego kids have hooked their first "big one" on an outing with dad or mom in a local lake. But many of San Diego's lakes offer much more than just fishing. Windsurfing, waterskiing, paddle boats, canoes, and rowboats can all be enjoyed on certain lakes; and many lakes are surrounded by playgrounds, ball fields, volleyball courts, horseshoe pits, picnic and barbecue areas, and trails to hike. Some also have camping facilities.

Fishing on all lakes requires a valid **California fishing license** for those 16 years old and up. You can purchase your license at most of the lakes described below, at most bait and tackle shops throughout the county, or directly from the Department of Fish and Game, State of California (4949 Viewridge Ave., 858-467-4201, Monday through Friday.) Cost is $27.55/year; a two-day license may be purchased for

$10.00. In addition, most lakes require a daily fishing permit. For San Diego City Lakes, the daily permit costs $5.00 for adults, $2.50 for children age 8 to 15, and free for children 7 and under with purchase of one adult permit.

The following entries represent only a partial list of lakes, selected for appeal to children. Devoted fishermen may have their own favorites that do not appear here; so much the better for keeping your special spot secret a little longer!

Note that, with the sole exception of Chollas Lake, which is open all year round, all of the lakes listed below are open for fishing and/or boating only during specified months. Call or visit the website listed below to confirm details.

San Diego City Lakes

Recorded information: 619-465-3474. Office of San Diego City Lakes: 619-668-2050 (www.ci.san-diego.ca.us/water).

☆ Lake Hodges (North County Inland)

From I-15 take the Via Rancho Parkway exit in Escondido and follow it west to Lake Drive. Turn left and proceed to the reservoir entrance.

Open for fishing Friday, Saturday, and Sunday from early March through October or November. Windsurfing is available from April to October. You can bring your own sailboard, or rent one at the lake for $5.00 for adults, $2.50 for kids 8-15.

This lake is surrounded by unspoiled hills with trails for hiking and mountain biking. The facilities are limited to a small bait-and-tackle shop that has restrooms and snacks, but the charming little town of Del Dios sits along the lake's edge and offers several restaurants for hungry fishermen. There is also a little wooden pier and a few picnic tables. This is a great bird-watching spot!

☆ Lake Murray (East County)

Phone: 619-668-2050. From I-8 take the Lake Murray Blvd exit; turn left on Kiowa Drive and follow to park entrance.

Open for fishing Wednesday, Saturday, and Sunday from early November to Labor Day. During fishing season, canoes and paddle boats are available for rent, along with rowboats and motorboats. (See Lake Miramar below for prices.) The Lake Murray area and its surrounding Mission Trails Regional Park is open all year for picnicking, walking, hiking, biking, and all-around enjoying.

This lake, along with the surrounding Mission Trails Regional Park, has been a favorite of local families for many years. **Fly casting lessons** are available to kids—as well as to adults—on Sunday mornings around 9:00. (For more information contact San Diego Fly Fishers through Stroud's Tackle Shop at 619-276-4822.) Besides the fish with which the lake is stocked, there are plenty of local ducks to watch, as well as picnic tables and barbecues. The trail that runs around the lake is paved and flat, and lends itself to bicycles, skateboards, or roller skates as well as strolling. Mission Trails Regional Park, just north of the lake, includes many lovely miles of hiking trails through undeveloped nature. (See Chapter 5 under the "Trails to Explore" section.)

Within the Mission Trails Regional Park area is **Cowles Mountain** which, at 1591 feet, is the highest point in the San Diego metropolitan area. Older kids will find this an easy "mountain climb," and will enjoy the idea that, having attained the summit, they are higher than anyone else in the region.

☆ San Vicente (East County)

From Highway 67 take the Vigilante Rd. exit and go east to Moreno Ave. Turn left on Moreno to the lake entrance.

Open Thursday through Sunday. From mid-May to mid-October, Saturdays and Sundays are for water-contact sports only (waterskiing, kneeboards, tubes.) From mid-October to mid-May, Saturdays and Sundays are for fishing only. Thursdays and Fridays are for both fishing and water-contact sports.

From October to May, this reservoir is a favorite with serious fishermen, although there are a few picnic tables for families who want to combine a picnic with a fishing expedition. From May to October, families who enjoy **water sports** congregate at San Vicente. It is the only city lake that has a slalom course for waterskiers; the use of this course is $10.00 per boat for a four-hour shift. You can rent waterskis, tubes, or kneeboards for $5.00 for adults, $2.50 for kids ages 8 to 15. A motorboat rental will run $32.00 for a full day, $24.00 for half a day (noon to sunset.)

☆ Otay Lakes (South County)

From I-805 take the Telegraph Canyon Road exit and follow it east to Wueste Road. Turn right on Wueste Road and follow it to the reservoir entrance.

Open Wednesday, Saturday, and Sunday from late January to early October for fishing, picnicking, and hiking.

This delightful South County getaway consists of two lakes, Upper Otay and Lower Otay. Permits can be purchased at Lower Otay Lake. **Fishing on both lakes is from the shore only and is purely catch-and-release.** These two factors lend a special charm to Otay Lakes: The sounds you hear will be primarily those of birds and wind and excited kids reeling in their fish—no motorboats disturb the peace of the lake. And catch-and-release is, for some youngsters, their preferred fishing method.

☆ Lake Miramar (San Diego)

From I-15 take the Mira Mesa Boulevard exit and go east on Mira Mesa Blvd. Turn right on Scripps Ranch Blvd, then left on Scripps Lake Drive to the entrance.

Open for fishing Saturday through Tuesday from early November to late September. In addition to the usual rowboats and motorboats often rented by fishermen, you can rent paddleboats and/or canoes here during fishing season. Canoes cost $5.00/hour. Paddleboats cost $8.00/hour for a two-seater, $10.00/hour for a four-seater. Note that

Lake Miramar is open all year for picnicking, walking, biking, or just relaxing.

This pleasant retreat, just 18 miles north of downtown San Diego, features family picnic areas and a concession stand where you can buy bait and tackle as well as snacks. Extensive hiking trails afford great views!

☆ Chollas Lake (San Diego)

From Highway 94, take the College Avenue exit, and go northwest on College one block to College Grove. Turn left on College Grove and follow it to the park entrance.
Open 6:30 A.M. to sunset seven days a week all year.

This is the only San Diego City Lake that is run by the Department of Parks and Recreation rather than by the Water Utilities Commission. As such, it is by far the most child-oriented lake in the county! In fact, **no one over the age of 16 is permitted to fish here**, so the competition is only between the kids and

the fish. There are **fishing derbies for junior fishermen** in the spring and in the fall, and there are periodic canoeing classes offered. The lake sits in a community park that is dotted with shady eucalyptus trees and picnic tables. There is **no charge for fishing here**, but registration is required.

There are no concession stands at Chollas Lake, so you must bring food for the fish as well as for the family.

Twice a month, kids can participate here in special programs to learn more about the natural world all around them. These programs are called "Nature in Your Neighborhood" and are free. On the second Saturday of the month, programs for the 5-year-old to-7-year-old set are offered; on the fourth Saturday of the month, the programs are geared for kids 8 and up. Call 619-527-7683 for more information.

Other Municipal Lakes

☆ Santee Lakes (East County)

Phone: 619-596-3141; from I-8, or Highway 52, 67, or 125, take Mission Gorge Road to Carlton Hills Blvd. Follow Carlton Hills Blvd to Carlton Oaks Drive, turn left on Carlton Oaks Drive and follow to the park entrance.

Open for fishing and boating 8:00 A.M. to sunset Monday through Thursday, 6:00 A.M. to sunset Friday through Sunday. Daily fishing permit $4.00 for adults, $2.00 for kids 7 to 15. Kids under the age of 7 fish free with an adult. Permits are available at the park office or at the general store.

Entrance fee: $2.00/vehicle on weekdays, $3.00/vehicle on Saturdays and Sundays. Discount for Santee residents.

Santee Lakes is a group of lakes, strung out in a long north-south chain. Besides all the fish you can catch, they offer rentals of rowboats, canoes, and pedal boats—great fun for younger kids. There are volleyball courts and horseshoe pits, as well as picnic tables and playgrounds. Unlike some other recreation areas, Santee Lakes' concession stands will even rent you the volleyball and horseshoe equipment!

There are facilities here for **family camping** and a swimming pool for the use of campers.

☆ Lake Poway (North County Inland)

Phone: 858-679-5466; from I-15 take Rancho Bernardo Rd. east for four miles (it becomes Espola Rd.) Turn left on Lake Poway Rd. and follow it to the park entrance.

Open for fishing and boating Wednesday through Sunday all year, 6:00 A.M. to sunset.

Fishing permits are $4.50 for adults 16 and up, $2.00 for kids 8-15, and free for children under 8 when fishing with an adult. Seniors 55 and older can fish for $2.00 on Thursdays. Boats are available for rent at the concession stand. Note that there is a $4.00 parking fee if you are not a resident of Poway.

If the fish aren't biting, you can rent a canoe, a paddle boat, or a rowboat ($8.00 per hour or $5.00 per half-hour.) Or you can enjoy the horseshoe pits, volleyball courts, softball diamond, archery range, and two playground areas. A three-mile trail around the lake makes a comfortable hike; afterward, take advantage of the picnic tables and barbecues. A primitive **campground** is available for individuals or groups.

In February, Lake Poway sponsors a **Youth Fishing Derby.** (See Appendix 1.) Call the above phone number for specifics.

Dixon Lake in Escondido

☆ Dixon Lake (North County Inland)

Phone: 760-839-4680; from I-15 take the El Norte Parkway exit in Escondido and go east to La Honda Drive. Turn right on La Honda and follow it to the park entrance.

Open for fishing, boating, and picnicking daily, 6:00 A.M. to dusk.

Fishing permits $5.00 for adults 16 and up, $3.00 for children 8-15. Children under 15 fish free with an adult. Seniors 60 and over pay $4.00. Call the above phone number for updated details. Note that there is a day-use fee.

Picnic tables and barbecues, playgrounds and horseshoe pits complement the bass, trout, and catfish that are Dixon Lake's main attraction. Even for the non-fishermen in your family, the nature trails, grassy meadows, and old shade trees make this a wonderful family picnic area. Rowboats and motorboats are available for rent, and there is also a **campground.** The newly opened Daley Ranch open space preserve forms the "back-

59

yard" of Dixon Lake, and makes for some of the region's finest hiking. (See Chapter 5 under the "Trails to Explore" section.)

County Lakes

Phone: 858-694-3049 for general information;
858-565-3600 for camping reservations.

☆ Lindo Lake (East County)

From Highway 67, take the Winter Gardens Blvd. exit. Turn left on Woodside Ave and proceed east to Lake entrance. Open for fishing and picnicking all year, 9:00 A.M. to 5:00 P.M. on weekdays, 9:30 A.M. to 7:00 P.M. on week-ends.

If the fish aren't biting, youngsters can watch the ducks, fly a kite, rent a pedal boat, or enjoy the playground. There is a softball field, tennis courts, and horseshoe pits along with picnic areas. This lake and its surrounding park are small, but delightfully pleasant.

☆ Lake Morena (East County)

From I-8 take the Buckman Springs Rd. exit, then south 4 miles to Oak Drive. Turn on Oak Drive and go west 3 miles to Lake Morena Drive.

The lake is well stocked with fish, and there is a large area in which to clean your catch. **Sailboarding** is also permitted on this lake, although you must have your own equipment. Motor and rowboats are available to rent, or you may launch your own boat. Hikers can pick up the Pacific Crest Trail where it passes directly through the park. **Campsites** are available, and there are two campsites **specifically designed for disabled people**. Wilderness **cabins** are also available for $25 per night, sleeping up to 8 people.

☆ Lake Jennings (East County)

> From Highway 67 in Lakeside, exit on Mapleview. Go east un-
> til Mapleview becomes Lake Jennings Park Rd. Watch for
> signs on the left to the park entrance. From I-8, take Lake
> Jennings Park Rd. north to the park entrance.
>
> Open for fishing Friday, Saturday, and Sunday from sun-
> rise to sunset. Fishing permits $4.75 for adults, $2.75 for
> kids 8 years old and up, and $4.50 for seniors 55 and up.
> Children under the age of 8 fish free with an adult.

If fishing is your thing, this is one of the best spots in the
county! Motorboats and rowboats are available for rent, and
the concession stand sells bait and snacks. The picnic area includes a **playground and horseshoe court.** In the summer
months, the lake stays open until midnight on Fridays and Saturdays for "Midnight Catfish Craze." On some Saturdays, the
ranger here leads nature walks through the trails that surround
the lake. Call 858-694-3049 for more information on the park.
Family camping is available.

☆ Guajome Lake

The County of San Diego also operates Guajome Lake, which
is mentioned in the section above under Guajome Regional
Park.

☆ Lake Cuyamaca (East County)

> Phone: 760-765-0515 or 619-447-8123 or
> www.lakecuyamaca.org; Take I-8 east toward Descanso,
> and exit on Highway 79. Follow Highway 79 north; the lake
> is at the northern end of Cuyamaca Rancho State Park.
>
> Fishing permits $4.75 for adults, $2.50 for children 8 to
> 15, free for children under 8.

Every Saturday morning at 10:00, the ranger offers a **free fishing class for kids**. *San Diego Union* writer and author Rich-
ard Louv calls it "far and away the best program for exposing
kids to fishing." During the summer, you can rent canoes and
paddle boats, in addition to the rowboats available throughout
fishing season. The lake is surrounded by a 3.5 mile hiking
trail; watch for the deer who regularly venture down to the lake.

There are barbecues, picnic tables, and **ample overnight camping** facilities throughout the park for those who want to make a weekend of it. Cuyamaca Rancho State Park is described in Chapter 5, "Adventures in Nature."

CHAPTER 5

Adventures in Nature

One of the many joys of living in San Diego County is the abundance of open space still remaining to be enjoyed by children of all ages. Even those in our county's most urban areas are never very far away from an adventure in nature.

The success of a nature adventure with kids depends upon our sensitivity to the child's capacities. Young children generally make enthusiastic hikers only when the hiking conditions are comfortable and brief. This may mean hiking only part of a trail, or planning many rest-stops. Be sure to bring along plenty of drinking water and plenty of snacks! For children up to 8 or 9 years of age, games to sharpen their "nature senses" may keep up interest (for example, "Who Can Find the First Blue Flower?" or "How Many Birds Can You See in That Tree?")

The following listing is, as always in this book, not meant to be complete, but represents a selected sample of adventures especially suited to children and their families. And, as always, we encourage you to do your own family exploring and to make your own discoveries.

TRAILS TO EXPLORE

Many of these trails are suitable not only for hiking, but also for mountain biking (for those families that prefer wheels to legs!)

There is a wonderful organization called the Canyoneers that sponsors docent-led hikes in many of the open spaces described

Remember that, especially in the case of open-space preserves, there are no rest-rooms or snack bars, so plan accordingly.

below. Call them at 619-232-3821, ext. 203 for details of upcoming adventures. The Sierra Club, at 619-299-1743, also sponsors hikes, many of them family oriented.

☆ Wilderness Gardens Preserve (North County Inland)

Phone: 760-742-1631; From I-15, take Highway 76; go east 10 miles to the entrance.
    Hours: Open Thursday through Monday, 8:00 A.M. to 4:00 P.M. Closed during the month of August

The San Luis Rey River meanders through the area, and you can still find crayfish in its waters; some claim they make the best bait for fishing in the pond nearby. Kids enjoy the **"Sensory Trail," designed** for visually-impaired visitors, but stimulating for everyone.

☆ Daley Ranch (North County Inland)

Phone: 760-737-6266; from I-15 take El Norte Parkway exit in Escondido and head east. At La Honda Drive, turn left and follow to the entrance.

This is one of San Diego County's newest open space preserves. It offers miles of trails through unspoiled country where you can find the native flora and fauna of inland San Diego County, and three year-round ponds where kids can look for tadpoles in the spring. Trails range in length from 1.4 to 5.5 miles. Call 760-839-4680 for information on docent-led outings.

☆ Elfin Forest Recreational Reserve (North County Inland)

Phone: 760-753-6466 Ext. 147; from I-15 take the Valley Parkway exit in Escondido and head southwest to Auto Park Way. Turn right and proceed to Howard Rd. Turn left on Howard and then right on Harmony Grove Rd. Follow its twistings and turnings to the reserve's entrance.

Like Daley Ranch above, Elfin Forest is one of the county's newest additions to open space preserves. Here you'll find at least three different habitats (chaparral, coastal sage scrub, and riparian.) You can pick up a Botanical Trail Guide that takes you through 27 specific "nature stops" and helps you identify what you're seeing. Unlike some of the other reserves, this one offers **picnic tables and port-a-potties.**

☆ San Dieguito River Valley Park (Includes many geographic areas)

Phone: 858-674-2275.

Designed to preserve a habitat corridor all along the course of the San Dieguito River, this park stretches from Vulcan Mountain, near Julian, to "Dog Beach" in Del Mar where the San Dieguito River meets the Pacific Ocean. One section of it has been designated as a **Children's Interpretive Walk.** (North County Inland area.) This trail includes fifteen "discovery points" described for children in a free booklet available at the trailhead. It covers a total of two miles, but you can turn around at any point. To find the Children's Interpretive Walk (also known as the Highland Valley Trail) exit I-15 at West Bernardo Drive/Highland Valley Road. Go left on Highland Valley Road, then make a quick right into the dirt parking lot where you will find the trailhead and the free interpretive material.

Another easily accessible section of the park for general family hiking or biking is the section between Escondido and Del Dios. From I-15 take the Via Rancho Parkway exit and go east to the first stop light (Sunset). Turn right on Sunset and follow to the small parking lot and trailhead. Here, you will skirt beautiful Lake Hodges where you can spot great blue herons, egrets, swallows, ducks, and sometimes in the winter months Canadian geese.

Frequent docent-led hikes cover all portions of the park. Call the above phone number for details.

☆ Blue Sky Ecological Reserve (North County Inland)

Phone: 858-679-5469; from I-15, take the Rancho Bernardo Road exit and head east. Rancho Bernardo Road will become Espola Road. Just after the road makes a sharp bend to the right, you will see the entrance to the reserve on your left.

There is a wide variety of habitats in Blue Sky, including a couple of small creeks that run through the area (usually dry during the summertime.) From the southern end of the preserve, you can look down on Lake Poway; from the eastern end, you can spot Ramona Lake and its dam.

Naturalist-led hikes are scheduled regularly. During the warmer months of the year, **family campfire programs** are offered; they include marshmallow roasting, singing, and entertainment. **Classes and special programs** for kids are also featured during the summer. Call the above number for details.

☆ Los Peñasquitos Canyon Preserve (North County Inland)

Phone: 858-484-3219; from I-15 take the Mercy Road exit. Go west to Black Mountain Rd.; watch for the parking lot.

The waterfall is a little more than three miles from the trailhead, making it a 6 ½ mile round trip hike— too long for most young kids.

This canyon encompasses the best of inland southern California with its streams, old shade trees, meadows and chaparral. During winter and spring, the small streams that traverse the canyon tumble down a series of boulders to the canyon floor, forming a little waterfall. This makes a great spot for a picnic. Small children will enjoy the shady stream with its stepping stones and abundant wildlife. Docent-led hikes are scheduled regularly; call the above phone number for details. A restored historic adobe rancho is at the east end of the canyon. Weekend tours are available.

☆ Iron Mountain (North County Inland)

No phone; from the intersection of Highway 67 and Poway Road, the trailhead is a few hundred feet south.

This 2,696-foot mountain in Poway is a hidden gem. The 3-mile trail ascends at a steady incline, but the moderate effort involved in the climb pays off with a spectacular view from the peak. A little mailbox at the top shelters the notes and mementos that climbers leave there. It makes for a delightful family outing; the sense of accomplishment upon reaching the top goes a long way toward building self esteem in young and old alike. Bring snacks and water!

A class trip at Quail Gardens

☆ Quail Gardens (North County Coastal)

Phone 760-436-3036; from I-5 take the Encinitas Blvd. exit; go east to Quail Gardens Drive and turn left; follow the signs to Quail Botanical Garderns.
Hours: 9:00 A.M. to 5:00 P.M. daily
Admission: Adults $5.00, Children 5-12 $2.00, Seniors $4.00. Children under 5 admitted free. Free admission 1st Tuesday of each month

Kids love this romantic oasis in the middle of Encinitas where you'll encounter nature on a kid-size scale. You don't have to undertake a long hike to find the waterfall and the lily pond below. The bamboo thicket, seen through a child's eyes, looks like a magical jungle, and exotic fruits hang from the many trees in the orchard. There's a tall wooden overlook from which children can see for miles.

Special children's tours, designed for the pre-school crowd, are offered on the first Tuesday of each month at 10:30 A.M. For the regularly scheduled docent-led tours for older kids and adults, call the above phone number.

At press time, plans are underway for the creation of a special Children's Garden. Check the news, or call Quail Gardens for updated information.

Ducks and kids at Buena Vista Lagoon

The ducks at Buena Vista Lagoon are so accustomed to being fed that they will swarm over anyone who sets foot on the little beach. We know one youngster who was terrified by this "duck attack" and refused to get out of the car. Be prepared!

☆ North County Lagoons (North County Coastal)

The string of lagoons that adorn North County's coastline are home to a wide variety of local birds, migratory fowl, and other wetland creatures. Some of the lagoons have been set aside as nature preserves or have continued to resist the pressures of development. They are unique environments, well worth a visit. Below is a listing of those lagoons most accessible to families.

- **Buena Vista Lagoon**
  From Highway 78 take the Jefferson St. exit in Carlsbad and head south. There is a little grassy park with benches and a "duck-feeding station" where many generations of North County youngsters have gotten to know their feathered friends. Sitting as it does just next door to the Plaza Camino Real Shopping Mall, this is a peaceful oasis in an increasingly urbanized area.

- **Batiquitos Lagoon**
  (760-943-7583 or 760-845-3501 or www.batiquitosfoundation. org). From I-5 take the Poinsettia Lane exit in Carlsbad and head east. Turn right on Batiquitos Drive, then right again on Gabbiano Lane. Park in the parking lot and walk past the fenced desiltation basin to the Information Center and trailhead.
  This is one of the North County lagoons that have been declared ecological reserves, and a well-maintained nature

trail winds along the lagoon's north shore for almost two miles. There are frequent naturalist-led walks on weekends; call either one of the above phone numbers for details.

- **San Elijo Lagoon**

    760-436-3944 or www.sanelijo.org. From I-5 take the Manchester Ave. exit and go east. In about a quarter of a mile you will come to a small dirt parking lot just across from the preserve entrance.

    This is an **easy trail**, winding its way along the southern edge of the lagoon and ending with a spectacular view of the ocean. **Signs along the way** help kids understand what they are seeing. There is a free nature walk on the second Saturday of each month starting at 9:00 A.M. These walks are led by docents from the Chula Vista Nature Interpretive Center (described below.) Call them for details at 619-409-5900.

☆ Torrey Pines State Park (San Diego)

Phone: 858-755-2063; from I-5 take Carmel Valley Rd. west, then go south on the coast highway to the park entrance.
Admission: $4.00 per vehicle.
Hours: Open daily, 9:00 A.M. to sunset.

The Torrey Pine tree is the rarest pine tree in the country; it grows in only one other location, Santa Rosa Island off the coast of California. These magnificent trees, with their twisted, wind-sculpted shapes, welcome visitors here at Torrey Pines State Park. There are several trails to follow, ranging from short and flat to long and steep; all of them are rich with the sweet aromas of sage and pine mixed with the sea breeze. One of the trails leads down to the beach below; this is a fine adventure for older children, but not recommended for small tykes because of the steep descent. Check out the indigenous plant garden, where "hands-on" is encouraged, and kids can touch and smell native plants.

The Visitors' Center, located by the parking lot, has literature on the park and maps of all the trails, as well as labeled exhibits of the flora and fauna of Torrey Pines. Docents lead public tours of the park each Saturday and Sunday at 11:30 A.M. and 1:30 P.M.

There are restrooms and water fountains outside the Visitors' Center only. Picnicking is prohibited in the park, but is allowed on the beach below.

Hiking in Torrey Pines State Park

☆ Bayside Trail at Cabrillo National Monument (San Diego)

Phone: 619-557-5450; from I-8, take the Rosecrans exit. Go west on Rosecrans; it becomes Highway 209. Continue west to the end.

Admission: $5.00 per vehicle; $2.00 for walkers, bicyclists, or city-bus-riders.

Hours: Open daily 9:00 A.M. to 5:15 P.M.

From the lighthouse, a 2-mile bayside trail descends through native sage, cactus, and yucca. In April and May, the trails are a special treat, bursting with spring wildflowers as well. The view is lovely; at some points you may find yourself higher than the pelicans and seagulls! With a little luck, young explorers may see a California sea lion sunbathing on the rocks.

The Visitors' Center, located by the lighthouse, sells brochures that, in addition to descriptions of local wildlife, include historical information.

The Cabrillo National Monument is mentioned in several other sections of this book. It is a wonderful spot for exploring tide pools and an easy vantage point for whale watching, as well as a fascinating piece of California history. You may want to combine several adventures into one here; or, better still,

70

come back at various seasons of the year to fully appreciate the National Monument and its surroundings.

☆ Famosa Slough (San Diego)

> **Phone: 619-224-4591 or www.groups.sandiegoinsider. com/ffs; from I-8 take the Sports Arena Blvd. exit. Go left on Sports Arena, then right on West Pont Loma Boulevard to Famosa Boulevard. Turn right and look for the wooden kiosk.**

The flat half-mile trail along this wetland is an **easy stroll** for even very young children, and the bird-watching is terrific: stilts, egrets, herons, and seagulls wade and glide through this fine wetland habitat. On the third Saturday of each month, guided walks depart at 1:00 from the kiosk on Famosa Boulevard.

☆ Mission Trails Regional Park, Mission Dam (East County)

> **Phone: 619-668-3275; from I-8 take the Mission Gorge exit and proceed northeast to Junipero Serra Trail; turn left and look for the sign on the left after about 1.5 miles.**
> **Hours: Open daily, sunrise to sunset.**

There are lots of shady spots for picnics by the stream, but be sure to watch for poison oak!

Staff members from the Visitors' Center offer guided walks daily. There are also regularly-scheduled **family campfire programs** in the amphitheater presented by the Park Rangers, and special **children's classes** during the summer. Call the above phone number for details. The old Mission Dam tames the San Diego River, which forms quiet, shaded pools in which young explorers love to splash. There is a spot where the water can be crossed on an old log; kids feel like real adventurers balancing themselves over the stream. The walking here is easy and peaceful, especially suited to young children and their families.

For older kids, **Cowles Mountain** is a must-do. It's the highest point in the city of San Diego (almost 1,600 feet), and can be scaled in a 3-mile series of switchbacks. The view from the top is worth the climb. If Cowles Mountain is your destination, follow Mission Gorge Rd. (see directions above) past Junipero Serra Trail to Golfcrest Road—about 5 miles. Turn right and up the hill for one mile.

Chapter 7 describes the Mission itself in more detail. You might choose to combine an educational visit to the Mission with a relaxing stroll along by the dam, although each experience makes a fine outing on its own.

☆ Mast Park (East County)

Phone: 619-258-4100, ext. 222; from Highway 52 take the Mission Gorge Rd. exit and go east (right) to Carlton Hills Blvd. Turn left and proceed to the park entrance.

Like its larger cousin Mission Trails Regional Park, Mast Park sits on the San Diego River. Groves of shady sycamore trees add a special charm to this little gem of a park. The nature trail is flat and easy for children. There's a little wooden bridge spanning the river—who can resist jumping or skipping across a wooden bridge?—and there's even a playground in the "developed" portion of the park.

Being a wetland, this area floods easily; don't plan to visit in the days immediately following a rainstorm!

☆ Tijuana National Estuarine Reserve (South County)

Phone: 619-575-3613; from I-5 take the Coronado Ave. exit in Imperial Beach. Coronado Ave. becomes Imperial Beach Blvd; follow it west to 4th St. Turn left on 4th, then right on Caspian Way.

Hours: Visitors Center open Wednesday through Sunday, 10:00 A.M. to 5:00 P.M. Reserve open daily, 10:00 A.M. to 5:00 P.M.

Admission: free

This wild and lovely wetland is the largest remaining estuary in southern California and has been protected since 1982 as a National Reserve. A number of endangered bird species, including the romantic peregrine falcon, make their homes here, so bring a pair of binoculars and challenge your young naturalists to count the number of different creatures they can find along the 6 miles of flat trails.

Junior Ranger Programs for K-6th graders are offered free each Thursday from 3:15-4:45 P.M. Bird walks leave the Visitors' Center each Sunday at 9:00 A.M., and guided nature walks are held on the 2nd and 3rd Saturdays of each month, departing from 5th and Iris at 9:00 A.M.

You might want to visit the Chula Vista Nature Interpretive Center (see below) before hiking here. Its excellent educational exhibits will orient you and your kids to the salt marsh sights and sounds around you.

☆ Anza-Borrego Desert State Park (East County)

At 600,000 acres, this desert park is almost the size of the state of Rhode Island and would take a lifetime to fully explore. But if you're looking for a fine family day trip, especially in the spring, head east to the town of Borrego Springs. At the traffic circle in the center of town, go directly west to the Visitor Center (760-767-4205.) It's open from 9:00 A.M. to 5:00 P.M. daily from September through May. June through August, it's open on weekends and holidays only. There you'll find plenty of hiking maps and interpretive displays to orient you to the park.

Just a little north and west of the Visitor Center is the parking lot for the Borrego Palm Canyon Trail. It's about 1½ miles from the trailhead to the glorious palm oasis, and the hiking is relatively easy. The oasis at the trail's end delights with its waterfall and cool pools.

Anza-Borrego is also a popular area for family camping; consult *Campgrounds of San Diego County*, by Jeff Tyler, for information on state and county campsites here.

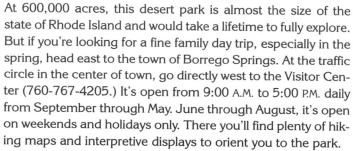

Remember that the desert, although extremely beautiful, is hot and dry, even when San Diego's coastal region is cool and damp. Bring hats, sunscreen, and plenty of water. And plan to go in the early spring, late fall, or winter. Avoid the desert in the summer if you can!

☆ Cuyamaca Rancho State Park (East County)

Phone: 760-765-0755; Highway 79, south of Highway 78 and north of I-8

Many families choose this spectacular park for weekend camping trips or for fishing expeditions (see Chapter 4). But if you just want a day of getting out into nature, you'll find lots of trails here, some perfect for even the smallest feet. There's a museum with Native American artifacts, a waterfall, and the ruins of an old gold mine.

For details on camping, consult California's state parks website at www.cal-parks.ca.gov. To make a camping reservation, call 1-800-444-PARK or go through the website of an organization called Reserve America at www.reserveamerica.

com. The state parks' basic fee structure is $8 to $12 per vehicle per night for developed sites, with $6 more for use of hook-ups to water, electricity, and/or sewer.

☆ Laguna National Forest (East County)

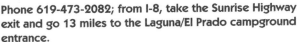

Phone 619-473-2082; from I-8, take the Sunrise Highway exit and go 13 miles to the Laguna/El Prado campground entrance.

A family outing to the snow in San Diego County's mountains makes for a wonderful winter adventure. But be sure to have tire chains in your car. and be sure to pack a warm change of clothes for everyone!

The Laguna National Forest is skirted by the Pacific Crest Trail, a spectacular adventure in nature high above the noise and smog of the world. For families wishing to camp here, sites are on a first-come, first-served basis; camping fees are $14 per family per night.

☆ Palomar Mountain (North Inland)

From Highway 76, take the Palomar Mountain turnoff (Highway S-6), and follow it to the top of the mountain.

From trout fishing in Doane Pond, to hiking, to enjoying a snow adventure in the winter, Palomar Mountain offers delights in all seasons. There are opportunities for family camping, as well, in Palomar Mountain State Park (760-742-3462) and the Cleveland National Forest (858-673-6180.) For fee and reservation information on the state park, see Cuyamaca Rancho State Park above. The Cleveland National Forest campground offers sites on a first-come-first-served basis; fees vary from $12 to $20 per night per family.

CREATURES TO MEET AND GREET

Kids have a natural affinity for other living creatures, be they furry or feathered or finned. San Diego is well known for its Zoo and Wild Animal Park, as well as for SeaWorld—all terrific destinations for critter contact. Those three are all covered in Chapter 1. But the suggestions below are for some lower key and less expensive family outings that include close encounters of the animal kind.

☆ Bates Nut Farm (North County Inland)

Phone: 760-749-3333; 15954 Woods Valley Rd., Valley Center. From I-15 take the Valley Parkway exit in Escondido. Follow Valley Parkway northeast; just past Lake Wohlford Drive, it becomes Valley Center Road (S6.) Follow Valley Center Road up the grade into Valley Center, and watch for Woods Valley Road on your right as you enter the town of Valley Center. Turn right. Bates Nut Farm will be on your left.
   Hours: 8:00 A.M. to 5:00 P.M. daily.
   Admission: free.

In addition to the creature opportunities listed below, watch for the dog shows, cat shows, and horse shows that are periodically featured in San Diego venues.

While their parents shop for nuts, dried fruits, and other country gifts, kids can pet the farmyard animals that inhabit this rural enclave. It's a wonderful place to bring a picnic lunch; picnic tables are provided. At Halloween families can pick their own pumpkin from the pumpkin patch.

☆ Fund for Animals Wildlife Rehabilitation Center (North County Inland)

Phone: 760-789-2324; 18740 Highland Valley Road, Ramona. From Highway 67, take the Highland Valley Road exit in Ramona and turn left.
   Hours: Open to the public Saturday and Sunday 10:00 A.M. to 4:00 P.M.
   Admission: free.

Most kids aren't aware of the wide variety of wild creatures with whom we share San Diego County. This center is dedicated to the rescue and medical treatment of injured animals including bobcats, mountain lions, coyotes, and birds of prey. Once the animals have recovered, they are released back into their native habitat. A visit here is a rare opportunity to glimpse some of our most magnificent neighbors.

☆ California Wolf Center (North County Inland)

760-765-0030, 619-234-WOLF, or www.californiawolfcenter. org ; P.O. Box 1389, Julian.

This is a place where animal lovers can see gray wolves and learn about their place in the environment. There are private tours set up by appointment Monday-Friday that last an hour, and they have a program that runs every Saturday at 2. The tours start at $25, and the Saturday program is $7 for adults and $3 for children. They will also come to schools and other organizations to teach about the North American Gray Wolf.

☆ Weidner's Gardens (North County Coastal)

Phone: 760-436-2194; 695 Normandy Rd. at Piraeus St., Leucadia. From I-5 exit on Leucadia Boulevard and go east between La Costa and Leucadia Boulevard. Travel north on the eastside frontage road (Piraeus.)
Open March 1 till Labor Day and November 1 to December 22.
Admission: free.

This is a family-owned nursery masquerading as a little farm. Kids can pet the goose, the goat, and the ponies while the rest of the family dig up their own tuberous begonias or pansies (and poinsettias in the winter season.)

☆ Monarch Butterfly Program (North County Coastal)

Phone: 760-944-7113; 450 Ocean View Ave., Encinitas. From I-5 take the Leucadia Boulevard exit and head west on Leucadia Boulevard. Turn left on Orpheus, then left again on Puebla, then right on Ocean View.
Hours: Saturday and Sunday 11:00 A.M. to 2:00 P.M.from late March to November.
Admission: Adults $3.00 , Children $1.50, Children under 6 free

This is a non-profit research facility that opens its doors to the public on weekends. You can hold a caterpillar in your hand, and you can see all the stages it will go through before it emerges as a butterfly. A dozen different butterfly species are on display; the staff is friendly and informative.

☆ Free Flight Aviary (North County Coastal)

Phone: 858-481-3148; 2132 Jimmy Durante Boulevard, Del Mar. From I-5 take the Via de la Valle exit in Del Mar and head west. Turn left on Jimmy Durante Boulevard and follow it past the racetrack.

Hours: 10:00 A.M. to 4:00 P.M. daily. Closed on holidays
and rainy days.
Admission: $1.00.

Owned by a veterinarian, this is actually a place to board or
purchase birds. But kids enjoy the squawks and chatter of the
scores of birds living freely in a semi-tropical aviary. The staff
will be happy to demonstrate techniques for holding a bird on
your arm or finger. You'll see parrots, macaws, cockatoos, and
other feathered friends, some of whom are incredibly verbal!

☆ Stephen Birch Aquarium-Museum (San Diego)

Phone: 858-534-3474 or www.aquarium.ucsd.edu; 2300 Expedition Way, La Jolla. From I-5 take the La Jolla Village
Drive exit and go west to Torrey Pines Road. Bear right
(north) at Torrey Pines and follow to Expedition Way, then
left on Expedition and follow the signs.
Hours: 9:00 A.M. to 5:00 P.M. daily.
Admission: Adults—$6.50, Juniors 13-17—$4.50,
Children 3-12—$3.50, Seniors 60 and up—$5.50, Children
under 3 and active-duty military—free.

The Birch Aquarium is part of the world-famous Scripps Institute of Oceanography. As such, its mission includes educating
the public about marine life. Tourists may go to SeaWorld
more often than to the aquarium, but among those who really
know and love the sea and her creatures, the aquarium is the
place to go. The oceanographic mu-
seum here is a more "personal" experience than is Sea World; it is smaller,
much less expensive, and can be
enjoyed in an hour or two.

From the minute they walk in,
kids are stimulated to look and to
see; signs challenge them to find and
identify particular fish as they work their way
from exhibit to exhibit. Even the smallest visitors get a thrill from being eye-to-eye with a
shark through the glass of a giant tank, and everyone enjoys
the hands-on tide pool exhibit on the terrace outside.

During the summer, naturalists from Scripps lead **snorkeling excursions** in the underwater

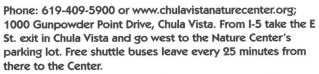

Light lunches and snacks are available on an outdoor patio in front of the entrance.

park near La Jolla cove, and **tidepooling excursions** are available all year. **Whale watching** excursions go out during "whale season," from December to March (See Chapter 3 under the section on Special Marine Adventures.) For further information on these adventures, as well as the many organized **classes offered to children**, call the phone number above.

☆ Chula Vista Nature Interpretive Center (South County)

Phone: 619-409-5900 or www.chulavistanaturecenter.org; 1000 Gunpowder Point Drive, Chula Vista. From I-5 take the E St. exit in Chula Vista and go west to the Nature Center's parking lot. Free shuttle buses leave every 25 minutes from there to the Center.

Hours: Tuesday through Sunday 10:00 A.M. to 5:00 P.M., Mondays from June through August.

Admission: Adults—$3.50, Kids 6 to 17— $1.00, seniors 65 and up—$2.50. Children under 6 free

You can't get to this Center without getting on a shuttle bus, so if you are pushing a baby stroller, make sure it's one that folds up quickly and easily.

Located on the Sweetwater Marsh National Wildlife Refuge, this is a wonderland for nature lovers. Even the shuttle bus ride is fun; you can see snowy egrets and blue herons as soon as you pass the gates that separate downtown Chula Vista from the wetland preserve. The entire Nature Center is completely child-oriented both in scale and concept: Almost every exhibit is "hands-on" and kid-sized. There is a petting tank full of small rays and sharks, and the center offers many **special events and classes**. Call for more information.

☆ Stein Family Farm (South County)

Phone: 619-477-4113; 1808 F. Ave., National City.
Hours: By reservation.
Admission: $2.00 per person.

The farmhouse on this working farm dates from 1890, and the original barn still stands. For local kids, it's an eye-opener to encounter the farmyard animals of their picture books right in the middle of town. Tours are usually available on a same-day basis. Call the above number for more information.

☆ Silverwood Wildlife Sanctuary (East County)

Phone: 619-443-2998; from Highway 67 in Lakeside, turn right on Mapleview and left on Ashwood. Follow Ashwood for 5 miles (it becomes Wildcat Canyon Rd.) Look for the yellow mailbox on the right side of the road.
Open Sundays only, 9:00 A.M. to 4:00 P.M. Closed in August.
Admission: free.

The San Diego Audobon Society runs this bird sanctuary, which is a wonderful place for kids to see native birds in their natural habitats. There's a shady bird watching area by the Director's house, and guided walks on Sundays at 10:00 and at 1:30. Bird watching is not for everyone, and younger children

Birds and bird watchers like quiet. If you have a child who is super-energetic, you might save your bird watching for pet stores!

will probably lose interest after a short time; bring a picnic, and combine "birding" with a relaxing outdoor lunch in this peaceful people sanctuary.

☆ Animal Stores (County-wide)

There are a number of stores in the county that offer an opportunity for kids to meet and greet the creatures of their choice. Check your local telephone directory for pet stores, or for specialty shops such as Reptile Haven in Oceanside, Bird Crazy in Clairemont, or the Crystal Blue Aquarium in North Park.

OTHER ADVENTURES IN NATURE

☆ Bell Gardens (North County Inland)

Phone: 760-749-6297 or www.bellgardensfarm.com; 15954 Woods Valley Rd., Valley Center. From I-15, exit Via Rancho Parkway in Escondido. Turn right and follow Via Rancho, which will become Bear Valley Parkway and then will bear right to become Valley Center Road. Once in Valley Center, turn left at the second stop light (Cole Grade Road) and look for the farm on your right in three miles.

Hours: Opening time is 10:00 A.M.; closing time varies with the season. Bell Gardens is closed on major holidays and rainy days.

Admission: $2.00 for children ages 4 and up Monday through Friday; free for everyone on Saturday and Sunday.

This is a working farm that you can explore by foot, by hayride, or by the little train that carries families around the property. On **weekends**, the hayride and train ride are both **free**, as is the admission. However, **reservations are required.** There's a produce stand where you can purchase the fruits of the season, and there are plenty of inviting shade trees for a family picnic. At Halloween, you can pick your own pumpkin from the field, and enjoy a walk through "Ghost Canyon!"

☆ "Nature in Your Neighborhood" at Chollas Community Park (San Diego)

Phone: 619-527-7683; 6350 College Grove Drive. From Highway 94, take the College Avenue exit and go northwest on College one block to College Grove. Turn left on College Grove and follow it to the park entrance.

Second and Fourth Saturdays, 10:00-11:00 A.M.
Free; no pre-registration required.

Park rangers guide children in hands-on nature discovery adventures right in the middle of the city through their "Nature in Your Neighborhood" program. The second Saturday of each month is for kids between 5 and 7; the fourth Saturday of each month is for kids 8 and above.

☆ Camping

A family camping trip can create lasting memories for everyone. Throughout this book local campgrounds are mentioned in their appropriate contexts (find beach camping in Chapter 3, park and lake camping in Chapter 4, mountain and desert camping in earlier sections of this chapter.) In addition to the campgrounds mentioned above, however, San Diego County has a number of private campgrounds that are worth mention-

A group campsite at Dixon Lake in Escondido

ing. One is the La Jolla Indian Campground on the San Luis Rey River; it is described in Chapter 10. Another is Rancho Corrido, nestled in the foothills of Palomar Mountain. This campground is a kid's paradise with a **stocked fishing pond reserved for the under 15 crowd, a playground, swimming pool**, and numerous activities (volleyball, basketball, horseshoes, shuffleboard, etc.) Fees are $19 per night for tent camping (two people) and $24 per night for RV camping (two people). There is an extra charge for each additional person. Call 760-742-3755 for details.

☆ Boy Scouts and Girl Scouts

Girl Scouts offers fun, exciting, and rewarding program opportunities for girls 5-17, from science and technology to sports and camping; from leadership skills and community involvement to career exploration and the arts. *Adult volunteer opportunities are available.* Contact the Girl Scouts, San Diego-Imperial Council, 1231 Upas St., San Diego 92103; 619-298-8391 or www.girlscoutssdi.org.

Boy Scouts offers a comprehensive character development program for boys grades 1-12 and teenage boys and girls. The program is designed to unite parents, neighborhoods, community leaders, and organizations with youth. The

81

Boy Scouts also offers three camps in San Diego. Contact the Boy Scouts of America, Desert Pacific Concil, 1207 Upas St., San Diego 92103; 619-298-6121 or www.bsadpc.org.

CHAPTER 6

Adventures in Town

San Diego has long been known for its temperate climate, its beautiful beaches, and its wide-open spaces. But in recent years San Diego has become an exciting urban center as well, with many of the advantages of a big city, including some entertaining shopping areas. Even when the shops themselves aren't particularly interesting to a child, many malls include features that can turn a shopping trip for Mom or Dad into a fun adventure for the rest of the family too. On a rainy day, when everyone has cabin fever, consider a short visit to a nearby pet store, or perhaps to one of the play areas provided in many of the major malls. Sometimes just an hour's outing can redeem an otherwise gloomy day.

For another kind of shopping adventure especially suited to children, consider the **farmers' markets, swap meets, and flea markets** held regularly in many areas of the county. The vendors are as varied as their wares, and most are extremely friendly. Kids can relate to this kind of personalized buying and selling; in fact, you may want to consider helping your children to set up a stand of their own at one of the swap meets after a major clean-up of a closet or a bedroom. Any kid who has traded Pokemon cards on the playground already understands the spirit of the marketplace!

Some of the malls listed below are outdoor malls, and some are indoor. Check ahead; an outdoor mall won't be much help on a rainy day!

San Diego

☆ Seaport Village

> Phone: 619-235-4013 or 619-235-4014 or www.spvillage.
> com; West Harbor Drive at Kettner Blvd. The San Diego trol-
> ley goes directly to Seaport Village.
>
> Open 10:00 A.M. to 9:00 P.M. September through May, till
> 10:00 P.M. June through August.
>
> There is a parking fee, but any purchase at all—even an
> ice cream cone—validates parking ticket.

Seaport Village is more than a shopping center; it is one of
San Diego's tourist attractions. The cluster of bayside shops
and restaurants are linked by walkways that are easy on small
feet and on baby strollers. Or, if you prefer, you can tour the
area in a **horse-drawn carriage** (young Cinderellas love this
attraction!) There are lots of casual snack bars where you can
sit outdoors and share your lunch with a seagull. Jugglers,
clowns, and other "street performers" stroll about providing
entertainment, especially on weekends and holidays. A beautiful old-fashioned **carousel** sends its ponies round and round

There's more than shopping at Seaport Village

photo by Susan Levy

84

to the music of its calliope; a trip to Seaport Village is hardly complete without at least one spin on this famous attraction ($1.00 per ride.) Other stores of special interest to kids include a kite store, a magic shop, and a "Fantasy World of Toys" (enter at your own risk!).

☆ Horton Plaza

Phone: 619-238-1596; Bounded by Broadway, First St., G St. and 4th Street.
Hours 10:00 A.M.- 9:00 P.M. Monday through Friday; till 7:00 P.M. Saturday; 11:00-6:00 Sunday.
There is a parking fee, but any purchase validates your parking ticket.

Horton Plaza is an open-air wonderland of shops, restaurants, novelties and entertainment. On the top floor, **entertainers** sing and perform—especially around holiday time. Shops of particular kid appeal include FAO Schwartz, the Warner Brothers Store, and the Disney Store. There's an international food court where you can find a tempting variety of snacks and meals in a family-friendly atmosphere.

☆ International Visitor Information Center

11 Horton Plaza at First & F Steet; 619-236-1212 or www. sandiego.org.

☆ Bazaar del Mundo

Phone: 619-296-3161; on Juan St. in Old Town State Park.
No parking fee.

An **international** shopping center built in Mexican Colonial style, Bazaar del Mundo features an inner courtyard surrounded by unique shops. This garden-like setting creates an atmosphere more peaceful than in some of the other centers; kids enjoy having an outdoor space in which to stretch and move while parents spend their money! There are **frequent performances** here, particularly of Latin American music and dance; once a year, a Latin American Festival is held in the courtyard (see Appendix 1). Gepetto's is a shop carrying international toys and children's clothing; this is fun for older kids.

☆ **University Town Center**

Phone: 858-546-8858; La Jolla Village Drive at Genesee between I-805 and I-5.
No parking fee.

Another open-air mall, UTC is supposedly modeled after a European village. One of the most unusual and fun features of this center is an **indoor ice skating rink**, open all year, where families can try their skill on ice. (See Chapter 9 for information on ice skating lessons for kids.) Even if you're not ready for the Olympics, you can watch others wheel and swoop (and fall!) while you eat your lunch from the safety of a balcony above the rink—a great source of entertainment. For parents with young children and serious shopping to do, this mall sometimes offers **drop-in child care**, charged at an hourly rate. This service is available at the Child-Time Children Center, a preschool located in the mall. If their regular preschool roster is not full, they can accommodate children from 18 months to 6 years Monday through Friday, and to 8 years on Saturday. Call 858-452-9732 for more information.

South County

☆ **Chula Vista Shopping Center**

Phone: 619-422-7500; H St. at 5th Ave. in Chula Vista.
No parking fee.

"Come for the carousel and stay for the shopping" might be the motto of this open air mall. Kids will, of course, love the two toy stores and the fast food restaurants, but the main attractions are the **carousel** and the glass elevator. A ride on the carousel costs $1.00.

East County

☆ **The Viejas Outlet Center**

Phone: 619-659-2070; 5005 Willows Rd. off I-8 (Alpine area).

Adults will love the discounted prices at this outlet center, and kids will enjoy the **level water fountain** in the courtyard that spurts water at regular intervals from flat holes. Put a bathing suit on your little one on a hot day, and let him/her play in the fountain while you shop till you drop!

North County Coastal

☆ Plaza Camino Real

Phone: 760-729-7927; 2525 El Camino Real, Carlsbad

This enclosed mall has all the usual stores, shops, and restaurants. But the particular attraction for kids is the two-story **perpetual motion machine** (conveniently located near the fast-food restaurants) where colored balls roll along moving tracks, dropping, disappearing, and reappearing in an endlessly fascinating pattern. Just to the west of the mall is the Buena Vista Lagoon where a little grassy park offers benches for weary grown-ups and water fowl for the entertainment of restless kids. (See Chapter 5.)

KIDS' CLUBS

Several of San Diego's malls offer Kids' Clubs as a special attraction for young children. These Kids' Clubs bring entertainers for an hour or so of free fun, usually in the main courtyard of the participating mall. The entertainers include Ms. Frizzle and her Magic School Bus from the San Diego Natural History Museum, children's educators from the San Diego Zoo, clowns, magicians, children's musicians, and more. As of press time, participating malls include Plaza Camino Real in Carlsbad (Kids' Club on Tuesdays at 10:15 A.M.); North County Fair in Escondido (Kids' Club on Wednesdays at 9:30 A.M.); and Plaza Bonita Shopping Center in Bonita (Kids' Club on Wednesdays at 3:30 P.M.) University Town Center in La Jolla offers Kids' Clubs during the summer months. These Westfield Malls offer evening programs as well. Call the mall (see phone number above) for details.

POKEMON/YUGIOH

Fans of Pokemon can join in local tournaments and other special events sponsored by the Wizards of the Coast Game Stores. Call the stores to request their events newsletter, or for information about upcoming tournaments. Wizards of the Coast Game Stores are in Mission Valley Center (San Diego) at 619-683-9490 and Plaza Bonita Mall (South County) at 619-470-9100.

SWAP MEETS AND FLEA MARKETS

San Diego

You might consider giving your children a set allowance to spend at a swap meet or flea market. It's amazing how quickly little 99-cent items can add up, especially if you have more than one child with you!

☆ Kobey's Swap Meet

Phone: 619-226-0650; 3500 Sports Arena Boulevard (parking lot of the San Diego Sports Arena).
Open Thursday through Sunday, 7:00 A.M. to 3:00 P.M.
Admission: Children under 12 free. For everyone else, admission is 50 cents on Thursday and Friday, $1.00 on Saturday and Sunday.

East County

☆ Spring Valley Swap Meet

Phone: 619-463-1194; 6377 Quarry Rd. near Sweetwater Rd.
Open Saturday and Sunday 7:00 A.M. to 3:00 P.M.
Admission: 50 cents for adults; children under 12 free.

☆ Santee Swap Meet

Phone: 619-449-7927; 10990 N. Woodside Ave. off Highway 67.
Open Saturday and Sunday 6:30 A.M. to 2:00 P.M.
Admission: 50 cents for adults; children under 12 free.

North County Inland

☆ Escondido Swap Meet

Phone: 760-745-3100; 635 W. Mission Ave. near Quince St. in Escondido.
  Open Wednesday through Sunday, 7:00 A.M. to 4:00 P.M.
  Admission: 50 cents on Wednesday and Saturday, 35 cents on Thursday, 75 cents on Sunday.

North County Coastal

☆ Oceanside Drive-in Swap Meet

Phone: 760-757-5286; 3480 Mission Avenue, Oceanside
  Open 6:00 A.M. to 3:00 P.M. Friday through Sunday (and holiday Mondays)
  Admission: 50 cents on Saturday, 75 cents on Sunday.

☆ Seaside Bazaar

No phone; First Street in Encinitas, one block south of Encinitas Boulevard.
  Weekends, hours flexible.
  Admission: free.

SOUTH COUNTY

☆ Kobey's Marketplace

Phone: 619-523-2700; 2050 Otay Valley Road, Chula Vista (parking lot of Coors Amphitheater).
  Open Saturdays and Sundays, 7:00 A.M. to 3:00 P.M.
  Admission: free for children 12 and under, $1.00 for all others.

☆ National City Swap Meet

Phone: 619-477-2203; 3200 D. Avenue, National City (parking lot of the Harbor Drive-in Theater).
  Open Saturdays and Sundays 7:00 A.M. to 3:00 P.M.
  Admission: 50 cents.

FARMERS' MARKETS

There are almost thirty Certified Farmers' Markets in San Diego County. Not only are they great places to pick up fresh produce, but they also provide free entertainment for little ones, as many offer kid-friendly activities such as performances by local dance classes and llama rides. (Yes, that's llama, as in the furry animals that live in the Andes! There is a llama farm in Valley Center.) Below is a listing, by region, of the major Farmers' Markets.

☆ San Diego

- **Hillcrest** Normal St. and Lincoln Ave. (DMV lot), Sundays 9:00 A.M. to noon.
- **Linda Vista** Mesa College Drive and Linda Vista Rd., Saturdays 2:00 P.M. to 5:00 P.M.
- **Mission Valley** Hazard Center (Friars Road just east of Highway 163), Thursdays 3:00 P.M. to 6:30 P.M.
- **Talmadge** "The Boulevard" at Marlborough St., Sundays 10:00 A.M. to 2:00 P.M.
- **Trolley Stop** Euclid Avenue and Market, Saturdays 1:30 to 4:30 P.M.
- **Ocean Beach** Newport Ave. west of Sunset Cliffs Blvd., Wednesdays 4:00 P.M. to 7:00 P.M.
- **Pacific Beach** Pacific Beach Drive and Reed Ave., Saturdays 8:00 A.M. to noon.

☆ East County

- **Alpine Frosty Acres** 3905 Alpine Blvd., Friday to Monday, mornings to mid-afternoon (closed November to April).
- **El Cajon** 4300 Marlboro Drive, Sundays 10:00 A.M. to 2:00 P.M.
- **El Cajon** 200 block of Douglas St., Wednesdays 10:00 A.M. to 2:00 P.M.
- **La Mesa** 800 block of Allison Ave., Fridays 3:00 P.M.- 6:00 P.M.

☆ South County

- **Chula Vista** E St. at Third Ave., Thursdays 3:00 P.M. to 6:00 P.M.
- **Coronado** First and B Streets at the Ferry Landing, Tuesdays 2:30 to 6:00 P.M.
- Coronado Loews Coronado, Terrace, Fridays 5:00 P.M.- 8:00 P.M.

☆ North County Inland

- **Borrego Springs** Christmas Circle and Palm Canyon Drive, Fridays 9:00 A.M. to noon.

- **Escondido** Grand Avenue between Broadway and Kalmia St., Tuesdays 3:00 to 8:00 P.M.
- **Fallbrook** Alvarado and Main Street, Fridays 9:00 A.M. to 1:00 P.M.
- **Julian** 2907 Washington Drive, Fridays 3:00 P.M. to 7:00 P.M.
- **Poway** 14050 Midland Rd.(Old Poway Park), Saturdays 8:00 A.M. to 11:00 A.M.
- **Rancho Bernardo** 13330 Paseo del Verano Norte (at the Bernardo Winery), Fridays 9:00 A.M. to noon.

☆ North County Coastal

- **Carlsbad** Roosevelt near Carlsbad Village Drive, Wednesdays 2:00 P.M. to 6:00 P.M.

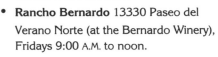

- **Del Mar** 1050 Camino del Mar (City Hall parking lot), Saturdays 1:00 P.M. to 4:00 P.M.
- **Encinitas** First street at H, Fridays 3:00 P.M. to 6:00 P.M.
- **Solana Beach** Lomas Santa Fe Drive and Cedros Ave., Sundays, 2:00 P.M. to 5:00 P.M.
- **Oceanside** Pier View and Pacific Coast Hwy, Thursdays 9:00 A.M. to 12:30 P.M.

- **Vista** Escondido Ave. and Eucalyptus Ave. (behind City Hall), Saturdays 8:00 to 11:00 A.M.

OTHER ADVENTURES IN TOWN

As always, the list of adventures with kids is bounded only by the limits of your imagination. We have discovered a few commercial establishments that bear mentioning by reason of their entertainment value. This is certainly not meant to be an all-inclusive list; in an area as large as San Diego County, we can't possibly have discovered every urban gem!

Bookstores and Libraries

Most bookstores (and virtually all public libraries) offer "story times" for youngsters. We cover this in more detail in Chapter 8, but check with your local bookstores and/or libraries, or watch for announcements in *San Diego Family Magazine* or *San Diego Parent* (both free publications available at public libraries and at many family-oriented businesses.)

Toy Stores

Some toy stores have regularly scheduled activities for children, such as crafts, music-making, or mini-classes. Most of these toy stores tend to allow more hands-on exploration of the merchandise than large chains like Toys "R" Us. A few such stores follow:

☆ **Whiz Kid Learning Materials**

**14168 Poway Rd., Poway
858-679-0506**

☆ **Zany Brainy**

1530 Camino de la Reina, Mission Valley (San Diego); 619-291-9500.

10661 Westview Parkway, Mira Mesa (San Diego); 858-547-8700.

5475 Grossmont Center Drive (East County); 619-466-6751.

☆ The Lakeshore Learning Store (San Diego)

Hazard Center, Mission Valley (Friars Rd. just east of Highway 163); 619-297-8494.

☆ The Learning Express

Del Mar Highlands Town Center, 3435 Del Mar Heights Rd., San Diego; 858-350-9039.

5630 Paseo del Norte, #116, Carlsbad (North County Coastal); 760-918-9275.

Other Stores

☆ The Basic Brown Bear Factory (San Diego)

2375 San Diego Ave. in Old Town; 877-234-2327 or www.basicbrownbear.com.

☆ Teddy Crafters (North County Inland)

North County Fair, Escondido; 760-291-1100

These are more like a total experience than like stores. You can design, stuff, and dress your own teddy bear, choosing from 30 different characters and 40 different outfits.

☆ Knorr Candle Factory (North County Coastal)

14906 Via de la Valle (east of I-5); 858-755-2051 or www.delmarcandles.com.

Call Knorr ahead to make sure that the beehive is functioning. Mother Nature is as moody as a four-year-old who's been promised a working beehive only to discover that the Queen Bee has died!

They really make candles at this candle factory, and you can see the process all the way from the beehive to the finished product. There are candle-making workshops for older kids (14 and up), but the younger ones will enjoy the little museum with great close-up photos of bees and hives, as well as educational texts on the life-cycle of these amazing insects. If you're interested, you can also see a real working beehive. The staff is very kid-friendly.

Miscellaneous adventures

☆ Dr. Martin Luther King, Jr. Promenade (San Diego)

Between Market St. and Fifth Avenue at Harbor Drive.

Built to honor one of America's greatest native sons, this urban park features stone pavers engraved with quotations from Dr. King. There is a beautiful water sculpture with open play spaces for children. When your kids have a day off from school for Dr. King's birthday, why not remind them of his legacy by taking a picnic lunch here and reading some of his words together?

☆ Tea parties

Do you have a little one who likes to create make-believe tea parties? Give him or her a taste of the real thing. The following options are pricey enough to fall into the "very-special-occasion" category. But for the right child, an opportunity to dress up in his or her finest duds and play prince or princess could be a life-long memory.

In San Diego, the venerable U.S. Grant Hotel puts on an elegant tea party in the main lobby Tuesdays through Saturdays from 2:00 P.M. to 5:00 P.M., complete with Royal Albert bone china, loose leaf tea (no tea bags!) and luscious finger foods. **Admission** is $14 for adults, $7 for children 5 and under. Reservations are required. Call 619-232-3121, extension 1512.

In the **North County Coastal** area, you can have the same experience at the Aviara Four Seasons Resort in Carlsbad every afternoon from 2:00 to 4:30. Cost is $16.50 per person. Call 760-603-3773 for reservations.

During holidays (Easter week, Christmas week, and Thanksgiving weekend), the Westgate Hotel in San Diego puts on a daily children's tea party. For the price of admission, you get an hour's tea and goodies followed by a second hour of stories told by a professional storyteller, plus little gifts. Prices are

$16.95 for adults, $10.95 for children ages 4 years to 12 years. Call 619-238-1818 for more information and reservations.

Other tea parties can be enjoyed in various locations around the country. They include Cobblestone Cottage Tea Shop at 1945 Alpine Blvd. in Alpine (619-445-6064); Julian Tea and Cottage Arts at 2124 Third St. in Julian (760-765-0832); and Mrs. Burton's Tea Room at 2465 Heritage Park Row, San Diego (619-294-4600).

☆ Fashion Shows for Kids

In the late summer (usually August) and the late winter (usually February), Nordstrom previews its new season clothing for kids during a Saturday-morning fashion show in which the models are all local children. Parents of participating kids get 15% off all children's clothing during the day of the fashion show. To be a model, all your child has to do is show up! Call your local Nordstrom store for details.

☆ The Bridges of San Diego County (San Diego)

Okay, so they're not the covered bridges of Madison County, but how many cities boast wooden suspension bridges right in the middle of town? Take a break from the hustle-and-bustle

A modern footbridge in Hillcrest

95

and stroll across a bridge spanning a canyon; let your youngster look for birds in the nearby treetops or squirrels in the canyon below. One such bridge is at the foot of Quince Street (Quince and Third); another is at the foot of Spruce Street (Spruce and Front St.) Between Vermont St. and Hayes Avenue, there is a bridge with inspiring quotations inscribed along the way (definitions of the word *bridge*, for example.) Street parking is usually available near all three bridges.

☆ Cruisin' Grand (North County Inland)

Every Friday evening between April and September from 5:00 P.M. to 9:00 P.M., Grand Avenue in downtown Escondido becomes a showcase for vintage automobiles. From shiny '56 Chevys to pampered old Rolls Royces, they cruise up and down the street or sit proudly parked along both sides for all to admire. Outdoor tables and chairs, food stands along the street, and plenty of benches for sitting, make this an easy and delightful outing for the family. The atmosphere is relaxed and friendly, and the cars are amazing!

CHAPTER 7

Adventures in Time

Every child in San Diego County is surrounded by vivid reminders of California's colorful past and rich heritage. Before children are old enough to consider "history" a dirty word, they can experience our region's history as a series of lively stories and locales. When encountered in the context of a fun family outing that may include a picnic, a swim, or just a relaxing time together, "history" becomes for parents and kids alike what it really has always been—a fascinating adventure back in time.

SAN DIEGO

☆ Cabrillo National Monument

> 1800 Cabrillo Memorial Drive, San Diego; phone: 619-557-5450 or www.nps.gov/cabr/index.htm. From I-8, take the Rosecrans exit. Go west on Rosecrans; it becomes Highway 209. Continue west to the end.
> Open daily 9:00 A.M. to 5:15 P.M.
> Admission: $5.00 per vehicle, $2.00 per walk-in visitor. (Walk-ins include those who come by bicycle, by bus, or by foot.) One admission is good for a week.

Juan Rodriguez Cabrillo was a Portuguese explorer who arrived here in 1542, thus becoming the first European to set foot in the region we now call California. He is honored with this monument, where you will find exhibits, slide shows, and films about the early explorers. Nearby is the old Point Loma lighthouse, open to the public, and a fine adventure for young explorers. Cabrillo National Monument appears in several

Bring a picnic lunch; there's not much to eat here!

Cabrillo statue and a panoramic view of San Diego

contexts throughout this book: Its Bayside Trail is one the Adventures in Nature (Chapter 5); **the tide pools** are a great Beach Adventure (Chapter 3), and the nearby observation deck makes a wonderful spot for **whale watching** (Chapter 3).

☆ Serra Museum

2727 Presidio Drive, San Diego; Phone: 619-297-3258.
From I-8 take the Taylor St exit and follow Taylor to the entrance to Presidio Park. Turn left on Presidio Drive to the museum.
Open Friday through Sunday 10:00 A.M. to 4:30 P.M.
Admission: Adults $5.00; seniors, military, students, and AAA members $4.00; children 6 to 17 years $2.00. Children under 6 free.

Father Junipero Serra, a Franciscan priest, arrived in what is now San Diego in 1769 from what is now Mexico but was then New Spain. A Spanish fort was established on Presidio Hill, and a Catholic mission was built within its walls; thus, San Diego became the first outpost of European civilization in California. The mission was moved five years later to its current location (see below), but archaeological excavations continue at its original site, the spot upon which the Serra Museum now sits. You can check out the excavations and visit this charming

museum, with its artifacts from the lives of early European set-
tlers. Afterwards, try a **picnic in neighboring Presidio Park**
where your young historians can discharge their excess energy
by rolling down the grassy banks of the lawns.

☆ Mission San Diego de Alcalá

> 10818 San Diego Mission Rd., San Diego; Phone:
> 619-281-8449 or 619-283-7319. From I-15 take Friars Rd.
> east to Rancho Mission Rd; turn right and follow to San
> Diego Mission Rd; turn left; you will see the Mission on your
> left.
>   Open daily 9:00 A.M. to 5:00 P.M.
>   Donation: Adults $3.00; students $2.00; children 12
> years and under $1.00.

California's first Mission, after a rough beginning that included
an Indian uprising, eventually thrived. San Diego's Mission Valley in those days bloomed with vineyards and olive groves; cat-
tle and sheep grazed by the banks of the San Diego River. At
the restored Mission, the daily round of life as Father Serra
knew it comes alive. Cassette players are available for
self-guided tours. The **urrounding gardens make for a lovely
picnic spot.**

☆ Old Town State Historic Park

> Between San Diego Avenue and Twiggs Avenue in San
> Diego; Phone: 619-220-5422. From I-8, take the Taylor St.
> exit or the Morena Boulevard exit. From I-5, take the Old
> Town Avenue exit. Follow the signs to Old Town.
>   Open daily 10:00 to 5:00 P.M.
>   Admission: free.

From the early 1820s to the late 1870s, the area known as Old
Town was the heart of the San Diego community, although the
character of that community continued to change over those
years. In 1821, Mexico won its independence from Spain; San
Diego became part of the new nation of Mexico. There are a
number of buildings in Old Town that have been preserved
from that period, bringing to life our early Mexican heritage.
Forty-seven years later, at the end of the Mexican-American
War, San Diego became an American city, and there are some

buildings from that era as well, which impart something of the vitality of the Old West.

The **Visitor Center** is located at the Seeley Stables Musem. **Free walking tours** depart from the Visitor Center at 10:30 A.M. and 2:00 P.M. every day. The tour lasts for one hour; if your young companion is not up to it, you can always drop out early for a rest in one of the lovely restaurants in the Bazaar del Mundo.

A few of the high points of Old Town are described below.

You can create your own walking tour, based on your interests and your young-sters' stamina. The "Olde San Diego Gazette," a free souvenir guide available through-out the park, helps you create an easy self-guide d tour.

- **Casa de Estudillo**

  This old adobe hacienda belonged to a wealthy Mexican rancher during the 1830s and 1840s. It has been beautifully restored and furnished with the finest Mexican furniture of that period.

  Anyone who has read the novel *Ramona* by Helen Hunt Jackson will be enchanted by the information that the Casa de Estudillo was Ramona's home. (This story may or may not be historically accurate, but the building is certainly ro-mantic enough to convince any adventurers who choose to believe it!)

- **Casa de Machado-Stewart**

  Another authentic adobe, this two-room home is more modest than the Casa de Estudillo, and far more typical of the usual homes of the Mexican period. It, too, has been re-stored and furnished in the style of its era. It lacks the glam-our of the rich hacienda, but it glows with a homey charm of its own that kids can relate to.

- **Mason St. School**

  This one-room schoolhouse was San Diego's first public school building, built in 1865. The pot-bellied stove and old-fashion desks give kids a new appreciation for their own schools. For a dramatic example of how school used to be, your pupil can take his turn wearing the dunce cap, or check out the chart on the wall that describes the rules and the punishments of a bygone era: "Fighting at school—5 lashes. Boys and girls playing together—4 lashes. Coming to school with dirty hands and faces—2 lashes"!

- **Cowboy Museum**
  A local woodcarver has turned his talents to creating marvelous dioramas of cowboy life as it really was in our county a century ago. These are fascinating to young children, for whom the dioramas come to life.

- **Seeley Stables Museum**
  Old wagons and stagecoaches, including the old Julian-to-San Diego stage, are displayed here, along with children's toys from a century ago, photographs of real-life cowboys, Native American artifacts, and a short slide show on local history. Any child who likes Wild West movies will enjoy this attraction.

- **Whaley House**
  Phone: 619-297-7511.
  Open daily 10:00 to 4:30. Closed Tuesdays from October through May.
  Admission: Adults $4.00; children 5 years to 17 years $2.00; seniors 60 years and above $3.00.

  In 1856, Thomas Whaley, a San Francisco merchant, moved to San Diego and built the first brick house in Old Town, making the bricks from local clay. Just as the Estudillo Hacienda had been a center for social life in its day, the Whaley house became the social center of its own time. The curators of the Whaley House will be happy to entertain your children with stories of the ghost who is alleged to haunt the old mansion to this day.

☆ The Firehouse Museum

1572 Columbia St., San Diego; Phone: 619-232-FIRE. From I-5, take the Hawthorne exit and go west one block to Columbia.
Open Thursday and Friday 10:00 to 2:00, Saturday and Sunday 10:00 to 4:00.
Admission by donation.

Any child who has dreamed of becoming a fire fighter one day will enjoy this museum. The building itself is an old fire station, and it houses horse-drawn fire engines, steam fire engines, old water pumps and hoses, fire hats, and lanterns. There is even an old speaking trumpet through which the chief would shout his orders.

☆ The Maritime Museum

> 1306 North Harbor Drive, San Diego; Phone: 619-234-9153. From I-5, take the Front Street exit to Ash; go west on Ash to Harbor Drive; turn left and you will see the ships.
> Open daily 9:00 A.M. to 8:00 P.M.; open till 9:00 P.M. during the summer.
> Admission: Adults, $5.00; children 13 to 17 years, $4.00; children 6 years to 12 years, $2.00; children 5 years and under free.

Since its earliest days, San Diego has been a harbor town, and the Maritime Museum, comprising three old ships open to the public, is a monument to that sea-faring heritage. **The Medea** is a luxury yacht dating from 1904 which has been fully restored to her old-world elegance. **The Berkeley** is an old ferry built in 1898; she used to operate between Oakland and San Francisco, and currently houses a ship-model shop, among other things, which is fun for kids who have tried their hand at building model ships. The best-known ship at the Maritime Museum is the famous **Star of India**, a full-rigged tall sailing ship of 1863 vintage. It's easy to launch into a full-scale pirate fantasy when you hit the decks of this old beauty. From time to time, The Star of India offers **overnight adventures** (chaperoned, of course) in which kids can spend the night sleeping below decks in the hammocks used by the real sailors when this tall ship plowed the open seas.

☆ San Diego Historical Society Museum

> Casa de Balboa, Balboa Park; Phone: 619-232-6203.
> Open Tuesday through Sunday, 10:00 A.M. to 4:30 P.M.
> Admission: Adults $5; children ages 5 years to 12 years $2; children under 5 years free. Everyone admitted free on the second Tuesday of each month.

Worth a visit if you're in Balboa Park, this little museum has a permanent exhibit as well as changing exhibits. You'll see lots of fascinating old photos from San Diego's earliest days, as well as artifacts from the various epochs of the region's history.

☆ Computer Museum of America

> 640 C Street, San Diego. Phone: 619-235-8222 or
> www.computer-museum.org.
>> Open Tuesday through Saturday 10:00 A.M. to 5:00 P.M.
>> Admission: Call for admission prices.

The senior author of this book has a hard time grasping the fact that a computer museum can now qualify as an Adventure in Time. But this ever-changing museum actually has computing machines and calculators dating back more than a century. Hands-on exploration is encouraged, and—of course—there are lots of interactive exhibits. A great attraction for any child interested in computers.

EAST COUNTY

☆ San Diego Railway Museum

> 31123½ Highway 94, Campo; Phone: 619-595-3030 or
> www.sdrm.org. Take Highway 94 southeast toward the
> Campo area. When you cross the rail-
> road tracks, the museum will be just
> to the south.
>> Open daily (museum) 9:00 to
>> 5:00. Train rides weekends and
>> holidays, 11:00 A.M. and
>> 2:30 P.M.
>>> Admission:
>>> Adults, $10; se-
>>> niors/military,
>>> $8.00; children 6 to
>>> 12 years $3; kids 5
>>> and under free.

Put on your conductor's cap and climb aboard one of the vintage trains maintained by this museum to preserve the history of railroading in the Southwest. For kids of all ages, the 16-mile **train ride** through beautiful San Diego back country is well worth the trip to Campo (see Chapter 10.) In addition, you can browse exhibits from a romantic past of the iron rails. Although a few snacks are available at the station, you will be much happier bringing along a **picnic lunch** to eat aboard the train or in the picnic areas by the museum.

☆ Gaskill Stone Store and Museum

> 31130 South Highway 94, Campo; Phone: 619-478-5707.
> Open weekends and holidays 11:00 A.M. to 5:00 P.M.
> Admission: Adults $2, children free.

Dating from 1886 are the old general store, the post office, the stage coach station, and the community building. You'll hear tales of the shootout that took place here, when San Diego County was part of the Wild West!

☆ Motor Transport Museum

> 31949 Highway 94, Campo; Phone: 619-233-9707.
> Open on the second Saturday of each month from April to November, noon to 5:00 P.M.
> Admission: free.

If you have a truck fanatic in your family, then this unique museum will be a treat. Along with the **antique trucks** on display, you'll find lots of photos and literature about the history of trucks and trucking. The building itself is an old mill, dating from 1929, built to mill feldspar.

☆ Heritage of the Americas Museum

> 2952 Jamacha Rd., El Cajon (on the campus of Cuyamaca College); phone: 619-670-5194. Take Highway 94 to its junction with State Route 17, also called Jamacha Rd. Follow Jamacha east to the campus of Cuyamaca College.
> Open Tuesday through Friday, 10:00 A.M. to 4:00 P.M., Saturday 1:00 P.M. to 5:00 P.M.
> Admission: Adults $3, seniors $2, children under 12 years free.

This is a small but lovingly-collected display of the natural and cultural history of the Americas. It includes meteorites, fossils, and artifacts from America's indigenous people. The view from the hilltop on which the museum is situated is worth the trip to El Cajon.

☆ "The Spirit of Nightfire"

Viejas Outlet Center, 5000 Willows Road, Alpine; phone: 1-800-847-6537 or www.viejas.com. Take I-8 to Willows Road exit; turn left on Willows Road and go 1.5 miles. The Center is on the right.
Nightly from June through November, starting at 9:00 P.M. Admission: Free.

This is a sound-and-light show using water fountains and laser beams to recreate traditions of the Kumeyaay people, indigenous inhabitants of San Diego County and contemporary members of the San Diego community. It's a magical journey into the past that's a treat for the whole family.

☆ Barona Museum and Cultural Center

1054 Barona Road, Lakeside; phone: 619-443-7003. From Highway 67, take the Mapleview exit east, then turn left on Ashwood. Ashwood will become Wildcate Canyon Road, and Wildcat Canyon Road will become Barona Road.
Call for hours of operation.

A small but fascinating archaeology museum preserves some of the past history of the Barona band of Mission Indians. Like the other Native American groups in our county, the people of Barona have known and loved the area we call home for thousands of years.

☆ Air Force WW II Museum

545 Kenney St., Hangar G4 (Gillespie Field), El Cajon; 619-448-4505.
Call for hours and admission prices.

You can watch planes take off and land at Gillespie Field and treat your aviation buff to the museum's displays of vintage airplanes, as well as films, photos, and artifacts of aviation history.

NORTH COUNTY INLAND

☆ San Pasqual State Historic Park

15808 San Pasqual Valley Rd., Escondido; Phone: 760-737-2201: www.parks.ca.gov, go to the "Find a Park" link. From I-15 take the Via Rancho Parkway exit in Escondido and turn right; go to the high school and turn right on San Pasqual Road; follow to Route 78, and turn right, following the signs to the Wild Animal Park. One mile before you reach the Wild Animal Park, you will see the San Pasqual Visitor Center on your left.
Open Friday through Sunday 10:00 to 5:00.
Admission: free.

The Mexican-American War ended in 1848, with the surrender by Mexico to the United States of California, Texas, and New Mexico. But on December 6, 1846, the San Pasqual Valley was inhabited by a band of Ipai Indians and by a handful of Californio-Mexicans. On that night, and the following day, a battle took place between the local inhabitants and the U.S. Army that was trying to claim the land. It was the biggest battle ever to take place in California. A small museum commemorates this moment in our history; a self-guided nature trail affords a beautiful view of the valley and fine specimens of local flora. Several picnic tables are available.

The best time to visit with kids is the Sunday closest to December 6. Each year **the battle is re-enacted** with horses and sabers and muskets (no real ammunition.) It's hard to tell who enjoys the show more, the participants or the spectators!

Julian is quite crowded during autumn weekends. Be patient and be prepared for long waits in restaurants.

☆ Julian

There are two good websites for Julian: www.julianca.com and www.julianfun.com.

In the late 1860's, shortly after the end of the Civil War, gold was discovered in the hills near the present-day site of Julian, and the town grew up to serve the hundreds of prospectors who flocked to the area. The "gold fever" eventually burned itself out, but Julian has maintained its Old West flavor and is a fun place to visit for a reminder of that chapter in our past. During late September and early October, the **apple harvest** comes in; although

Julian tends to be crowded with tourists during those weeks, it's worth a trip to bring home a gallon of sweet cider, a bag of Julian apples, and a fresh apple pie. There are still a few small, privately-owned orchards that allow families to pick their own fruit. One of these is Calico Ranch. Call them for days and hours at 619-586-0392.

Kids enjoy touring the **Julian Pioneer Museum** (open Tuesday through Sunday from 10:00 A.M. to 4:00 P.M. from April through November. Phone 760 765-0227). The old **Julian Hotel**, originally built just after the Civil War by an entrepreneur who had been a former slave, is a wonderful example of western architecture of that time.

☆ Mission San Antonio de Pala and Cupa Cultural Center

Pala Mission Road on the Pala Indian Reservation (east of Oceanside); phone: 760-742-1590. Take Highway 76 east from I-15 to Pala Mission Rd. Follow Pala Mission Road 6 miles to the mission.

Hours: Mission museum open Tuesday through Sunday, 10:00 A.M. to 4:00 P.M. Cupa Cultural Center open Monday through Friday 8:00 A.M. to 4:30 P.M.

Admission: Mission museum—Adults $2, children $1; Cultural Center—free.

Nestled in one of San Diego County's most beautiful rural areas, this attraction on the Pala Reservation is a hidden gem. The mission was originally built in the early 1800s as an *assistencia* ("assistant") to its big sister Mission San Luis Rey. Like its big sister, it remains active today, with a school and a church. The chapel wall still glows with the original paintings, created by the ancestors of today's Cupa people. The gardens and the old cemetery retain the charm of two centuries ago.

The relationship between California's missions and California's native people has always been a complex one, and it is somehow fitting that the Cupa Cultural Center, celebrating the history of the Cupa band of Indians, should be situated right next to the mission. On the first weekend in May, you can bring the whole family to enjoy Native American dance, food, and arts and crafts at the annual Cupa Day Festival held at the Cultural Center (see Appendix 1).

☆ Deer Park Winery and Auto Museum

> 29013 Champagne Boulevard, Escondido; phone: 760-749-1666. Take I-15 to the Deer Springs Rd. exit in northern Escondido. Go east on Deer Springs Rd., then north (left) on Champagne Boulevard. Look for the winery on your left in three miles.
>   Open daily 10:00 A.M. to 4:00 P.M.
>   Admission (to museum): Adults $6, children under 12 free.

This attraction would be better dubbed "Museum of Americana." It does, indeed, feature a great collection of **vintage cars** (said to be one of the nation's largest collections of convertibles), but it also includes lots of other **American memorabilia**, including a Barbie room, old-time radios, and antique wine making equipment. The grounds, with their gazebos, orchards, and grape arbors, make a lovely place for a family picnic.

NORTH COUNTY COASTAL

☆ Mission San Luis Rey de Francia

> 4050 Mission Ave. Oceanside; Phone: 760-757-3651. Take Highway 76 to just east of El Camino Real. The mission will be on your left.
>   Museum open Monday through Saturday 10:00 A.M. to 4:30 P.M., Sunday 11:30 A.M. to 4:30 P.M.
>   Admission: free.

The eighteenth in the string of California missions, San Luis Rey is one of only four missions still being run by the Franciscan order. The ancient cemetery includes headstones from the year of the mission's establishment, 1798. The peaceful grounds hold the very first pepper tree in California, brought here from Peru in 1830 and still going strong. The museum displays early artwork, Native American artifacts, and historical memorabilia from the mission's colorful past.

☆ Antique Gas and Steam Engine Museum

2040 North Santa Fe Ave., Vista; Phone: 760-941-1791. From Highway 76, exit on Santa Fe Avenue and go two miles south.
Open daily 10:00 A.M. to 4:00 P.M.
Admission: Adults $3, children 12 years and under $2.

Some North County residents remember when this area was rural ranch land; a few still remember using the horse-drawn farm equipment and the gas and steam engines on display here. The best time to take kids is the third and fourth weekends in June and October. (See Appendix 1.) At those times, the engines are cranked up and operating, and there are exhibitions of black-smithing and log-sawing, along with folk dancing. The museum is in Guajome Park (see Chapter 5); you can combine a peaceful picnic in the park with a trip back in time.

☆ California Surf Museum

308 N. Pacific St. at Third St., Oceanside; 760-721-6876. From I-5 take the Mission Avenue exit in Oceanside and go west to Pacific Street. Turn right and look for the pier.
Open Monday, Thursday, Friday from noon to 4:00 P.M., weekends 10:00 A.M. to 4:00 P.M. During the summer, the museum is also open on Tuesdays and Wednesdays from noon to 4:00.
Admission: free; donations suggested.

Sitting atop the Oceanside Pier (naturally!), this low-key, fun museum preserves Pacific Rim surfing lore through photos, memorabilia, clothing, etc. The display changes every few months, so local families can make it an annual outing. This is a good adventure for wannabe surfers or surfer fans.

☆ Dinosaur Gallery

> 1327 Camino Del Mar, Del Mar; Phone: 858-794-4855. From I-5 take the Del Mar Heights exit to Camino Del Mar and turn right.
> Open daily 11:00 A.M. to 5:00 P.M.

Talk about adventures in time: How about going back about 25 million years or so? Check out the scores of fossils here, some of which your children are invited to touch as well as to view. Any budding paleontologist will get a kick out of this little gallery.

This is not a museum, but a for-profit store. Take only those kids that you know you can keep a close eye on.

☆ The Museum of Making Music

> 5790 Armada Drive, Carlsbad (just east of LEGOLAND); Phone: 877-551-9976 or www.museumofmakingmusic.com. From I-5 take the Cannon Drive exit. Go east to Legoland Drive and turn right. Stay to the right of the traffic circle, and you will be on Armada Drive. Go about half a mile and look for the building with the big green dome.
> Open Tuesday through Sunday 10:00 A.M. to 5:00 P.M.
> Admission: Adults $5; children ages 4-18 and students, seniors, active military $3; children 3 years and under free.

This unique museum covers a century of American music making and includes vintage instruments, samplings of popular music from each of the past ten decades, and historic photos. For kids, a highlight is the hands-on experience offered by the museum: Visitors are invited to play a digital keyboard, a guitar, various rhythm instruments, and even a violin.

SOUTH COUNTY

☆ Hotel del Coronado

> 1500 Orange Avenue, Coronado; phone: 619-435-6611. From I-5 take the Coronado Bridge exit. Follow the flow of traffic to Orange Avenue. Turn left on Orange and proceed

through town to the hotel, which will be on your right.
There is a fee for parking.
   Open daily.
   Admission: Free.

The "Hotel Del," as it is known to locals, is a venerable old dowager of San Diego County. The building itself is a trip back in time, preserving the atmosphere of Victorian elegance. One of the rooms is reputed to be haunted, and the hotel staff will be happy to regale you with the story. On the lower level, you can stroll through the Hall of History where old photos commemorate the various celebrities who have passed through the hotel's doors, including the entire cast of the famous movie *Some Like It Hot.*

☆ Sweetwater-Rohr Park Railroad

4548 Sweetwater Road, Bonita; phone: 619-422-3175.
From Highway 54, exit on Bonita Center Way in Bonita. Turn right on Sweetwater Road and follow it to Rohr Park.

On the second full weekend of each month, between 8:00 A.M. and 5:00 P.M., you can take a ride on an authentic **old steam locomotive** in lovely Rohr Park. This trip back in time is sponsored by the Chula Vista Live Steamers, Inc., and they request a 25 cent donation for their efforts—a real bargain!

LOCAL HISTORICAL SITES

Many communities have preserved their local history in heritage parks, historical buildings, or a combination of the above. They are all worth a visit, especially if you live in the area. It's fun for children to see photos of their town as it was when Grandma and Grandpa were kids. A partial list of local adventures in time follows.

East County

- **Lakeside Historical Society**, 9906 Maine Avenue in Lakeside. 619-561-1886. **Admission:** free. Features not only old photos, but a city block of many of the town's original buildings.

- **Bancroft Ranch House** Museum, 9050 Memory Lane, Spring Valley. 619-469-1480. **Admission:** free. Built at the time of the Civil War, this old house displays memorabilia of the area, including Native American artifacts.

North County Coastal

- **Vista Historical Museum**, 651 East Vista Way. 760-639-6164. **Admission:** free. Situated in Wildwood Park, the Vista Historical Museum recreates the area's history and the lifestyles of its diverse inhabitants. The museum is open Wednesday through Saturday from 10:00 to 3:00 and is free. Nearby, also in Wildwood Park, is the old **Rancho Buena Vista Adobe**, an old ranch house that is decorated in period furnishings and is a great example of the area's early ranch architecture. The Rancho Adobe is open during the same hours as the museum, but is also open Sundays from 12:30 to 3:00. **Admission** to the Adobe is $3 for adults, $2 for seniors and Vista residents, $1 for students, and 50 cents for children under 12 years. This admission price includes a guided tour. Wildwood Park itself has a play area for children, picnic tables, and fire rings.

- **Rancho Guajome Adobe**, 2210 North Santa Fe Avenue, Vista. 760-724-4082. This is another old ranch house, beautifully preserved and furnished. It is situated in Guajome Regional Park (see Chapter 5), a lovely spot for a family picnic. The Adobe is open Saturdays and Sundays only. Tours cost $2 for adults, $1 for children, and depart at 11:00, 12:30, and 2:30.

- **Heritage Park Village and Museum**, 220 Peyri Road, Oceanside. 760-433-8297. **Admission:** free. This is another adventure into the Old West. In the space of a city block, you'll see a blacksmith shop, an old school, a general store, an inn, and a private home from 1886. The buildings are open to the public Sundays only, from noon to 4:30.

- **San Dieguito Heritage Museum**, 561 South Vulcan Ave., Encinitas. 760-632-9711. **Admission:** free. A stagecoach sits in front of what was once a gas station. Inside, local history comes to life through artifacts from early Kumeyaay culture, old-fashioned toys, and a furnished hut from old Olivenhain. **Open** Wednesday through Saturday, 10:00 to 3:00.

North County Inland

* Escondido Historical Society's **Heritage Walk Museum Complex**, 321 North Broadway (in Grape Day Park), Escondido. 760-743-8207. **Admission:** free. A blacksmith shop, an old railroad depot, and an old Victorian house are some of the features of this complex designed to preserve Escondido's early days. Museum is **open** Thursday through Saturday, 1:00 P.M. to 4:00 P.M. The historic buildings are open to the public; special tours can be arranged.

* **Old Poway Park**, 14134 Midland Rd., Poway. 858 486 4063. Local farmers bring their produce to the old-style market square here on Saturday mornings. You and your kids can ride an **old steam locomotive** (vintage 1907), or an even older **trolley car** (vintage 1894.) The locomotive runs on the first and third weekends of the month, and the trolley car runs on the second and fourth weekends. Hours are 10:00 to 4:00 on Saturday and 11:00 to 2:00 on Sundays. The rides are 50 cents for children and $2 for adults on the locomotive, $1.50 for adults on the trolley. Other attractions include a replica of a passenger car from 1900 and four mining gondolas dating from 1883 and converted for passenger use. Pack a picnic and make a day of it!

There's a great old gazebo in Old Poway Park. If you have a performer in the family, bring some music along and give him/her center stage!

* **Ramona Pioneer Historical Society**, 645 Main St., Ramona. 760-789-7644. **Admission:** free. Early life in the old West is the focus in this restored complex of buildings which includes the Guy B. Woodward Museum of History and the Amy Strong Castle. Behind the old home is an authentic Dutch windmill. **Open** Thursday through Sunday 1:00 to 4:00 P.M.

South County

* **Kimball House**, 921 A Avenue, National City. 619-477-0859. **Admission:** free. National City's Heritage Square features this splendid 1889 home, built by the town's founding father,

Frank Kimball. The restoration and early furnishings are top quality. **Open** Sundays from dawn to dusk.

- **Bonita Museum and Cultural Center**, 4035 Bonita Rd., Bonita. 619-267-5141. **Admission:** free. This local museum is housed in an old fire station. Kids can view a classic old fire truck as well as photos and artifacts depicting the early days of the Bonita Valley. **Open** Thursday through Saturday, 10:00 to 3:00.

SPECIAL ADVENTURE IN TIME

Thousands of years before Cabrillo set foot on San Diego soil, the original inhabitants of our county fished its waters, climbed its mountains, and worked its deserts in the seasonal rounds of their lives. They left no buildings or monuments, but records of their culture are there for those who look. Any description of adventures in time would be incomplete without mention of the pictographs (rock paintings) and petroglyphs (rock carvings) which stand as messages to us from the earliest residents of our region. For families visiting the Anza-Borrego State Park (See Chapter 5), there is an easy trail to some fine pictographs which kids find exciting to "discover." Check the guidebook *The Anza-Borrego Desert Region,* by Lowell and Diana Lindsay for detailed directions to the pictographs in Little Blair Valley; or ask at the Visitors Center.

CHAPTER 8

Adventures of the Mind

Learning—it's what childhood is really all about, and it is the most exciting adventure of all. San Diego is full of opportunities to combine learning with fun; in fact, many of the adventures listed below allow adults to participate, too, so that learning together can become another family activity.

It has been impossible to include every learning opportunity that San Diego has to offer; check with your local Parks and Recreation Department, YMCA, library, and the yellow pages of your telephone directory for specific classes in your community.

☆ The Children's Museum/Museo de los Niños (San Diego)

The San Diego Children's Museum, a long-time favorite of generations of San Diego families, is closed for rebuilding as of press time. They plan to reopen in 2005. Meanwhile, they consider themselves to be a "museum without walls" and continue to offer periodic special events. When they do reopen, families will find this museum to offer wonderful interactive features including arts and crafts, science, and cross-border experiences. Call 619-233-KIDS for updated information.

☆ The Children's Discovery Museum (North County Coastal)

300 Carlsbad Village Drive, Suite 103, Carlsbad; phone: 760-720-0737; www.museumforchildren.org.

Open Tuesday through Thursday 12:00 noon to 5:00 P.M.; Friday and Saturday 10:00 A.M. to 5:00 P.M. and Sunday noon to 5:00. Closed Monday.

Admission: $4 for anyone over the age of 2.

The place is so big, and so diverse, that we advise bringing along an extra adult if you have children of different ages, so that everyone can enjoy his/her level.

This little museum offers a play supermarket where kids can select groceries, work the cash register, and push a cart just like Mommy and Daddy. There is a castle complete with dress-up clothes for little knights and princesses; there's a play boat with magnetic fish and fishing poles, and there are several crafts stations along with funhouse mirrors, giant bubbles, and more. It's close to the beach and close to several kid-friendly restaurants.

☆ Escondido Children's Musuem/Museo para Niños (North County Inland)

As of press time, the new Escondido Children's Museum is in its pilot year. Although they do not yet have a permanent home, you can visit them at their temporary home in Escondido at 156 West Grand Avenue. To find out more about this exciting new center, call 760-233-7755 or visit their website at www.escondidochildrensmuseum.org.

LIBRARIES

There are 32 libraries in the city of San Diego, and 31 more in the county, as well as in the cities of Carlsbad, Chula Vista, Coronado, Escondido, National City, and Oceanside. Almost every one of these libraries offers **wonderful adventures for children**, from bedtime story hours to films to special activities for holidays; some branches offer their programs in Spanish as well as English. Membership at the library is free, and it's probably the best deal in town for family entertainment. In addition to the story times and other special activities, you can borrow video and audio products for your children, and—of course—books! Most libraries also offer **free access to a computer**, including the internet, which can be a big bonus for families without a home computer. A child can get his/her very own library card simply by being able to write his/her name—a great motivator for learning this skill. Most branches have a children's librarian who will be eager to help you and your child make your selections. Check your phone book for the branch nearest you, and call for a listing of upcoming events for kids.

OTHER "STORY TIMES"

In addition to public libraries, a number of commercial establishments offer story times for children. These include most bookstores and some toy stores. A partial list follows; be sure to check for updated days and times.

Toy Stores

Note: The following stores offer story times and much, much more. Check their individual calendar of events for crafts, games, music, etc.

- **Learning Express** (North County Coastal)
  Del Mar Highlands Town Center, 3435 Del Mar Heights Rd.; 858-350-9039
  Carlsbad at 5630 Paseo del Norte, #116; 760-918-9275.

- **Lakeshore Learning Store (San Diego)**
  7510 Hazard Center Drive, San Diego; 619-297-8494.

- **Zany Brainy (San Diego and East County)**
  1530 Camino de la Reina, San Diego (Mission Valley); 619-291-9500.
  10661 Westview Parkway, San Diego (Mira Mesa); 858-547-8700.
  5475 Grossmont Center Drive, Suite B, La Mesa; 619-466-6751.

- **Trains are Good (San Diego)**
  2802 Juan Street, San Diego (Old Town) 619-294-8372.
  Features books and stories about trains, story time for tots on Tuesdays at 4:00 P.M.

Children's Book Stores

- **Prince & the Pauper Collectible Children's Books (San Diego)**
  3201 Adams Avenue, San Diego; 619-283-4380.
  This bookstore sells both new and used children's books and has a fun play area for kids.

- **The Yellow Book Road (East County)**
  8923 La Mesa Boulevard, La Mesa; 619-463-4900.
  This bookstore does not have regularly scheduled story times, but they do specialize in children's books and often have book signings and presentations by children's authors.

Major Bookstore Chains

☆ San Diego

- Barnes & Noble
  7610 Hazard Center Drive; 619-220-0175.
  Fridays, 7:00 P.M. "Pajamarama" (Kids can come in their P.J.'s to hear a few stories and browse the huge children's book department).

- Bookstar
  3150 Rosecrans Place; 619-225-0465;
  8650 Genesee Ave.; 858-457-7561.
  Mondays, 7:00 P.M. Story Hour

- Borders Books, Music, & Café
  1072 Camino del Rio North; 619-295-2201.
  Tuesday and Thursday at 10:30 A.M. is "Tot Time."

☆ North County Coastal

- Barnes & Noble
  12835 El Camino Real, Del Mar; 858-481-4038.
  Wednesday at 7:00 P.M. is a P.J. party; Saturday at 11:00 A.M. is another story time.

- Barnes & Noble
  1040 N. El Camino Real, Encinitas; 760-943-6400.

They have a Magic Tree House Book Group on the 2nd Friday of every month, a Newberry Award Winning Book Group on the 3rd Thursday of every month, and two story times, Saturdays at 11 and Tuesdays at 11.

- Barnes & Noble
  2615 Vista Way, Oceanside; 760-529-0106.
      Story times are at 7:00 P.M. on Fridays and at 2:00 P.M. on Saturdays.

☆ North County Inland

- Barnes & Noble
  810 W. Valley Parkway, Escondido; 760-480-2760.
      Wednesday 10:00 A.M.—special story time for the tiniest learners, featuring baby "board books."
      Mondays 7:00 P.M.—P.J. party with stories
      Note: This store offers other activities for children throughout the month; check their calendar of events.

- Barnes & Noble
  11744 Carmel Mountain Road, Rancho Peñasquitos; 858-674-1055.
      Stories at 10:30 A.M. on Tuesdays and Saturdays.

- Barnes & Noble
  10775 Westview Parkway, Mira Mesa; 858-684-3166.
      They have a parent and tot storytime on Thursdays at 10 A.M., a "pajamarama" on Fridays at 7:30 P.M., and a storytime at 11:30 on Saturdays.

- Borders Books and Music
  11160 Rancho Carmel Drive, Rancho Peñasquitos; 858-618-1814.
      Tuesdays and Wednesdays at 10:00 A.M. are "Tot Times." Story hour for older children is on Saturday at 3:00 P.M.
      Note: This store also offers other children's activities; check their calendar.

- Waldenbooks
  200 E. Valley Parkway, Escondido; 760-746-4859.
      Story time is on Wednesday morning at 11:00 A.M.

☆ East County

- Barnes & Noble
  5500 Grossmont Center Drive, La Mesa; 619-667-2870.
    Story times are at 10:00 A.M. on Monday and Wednesday
    and 7:00 P.M. on Friday.

- Barnes & Noble
  9938 Mission Gorge Rd., Santee; 619-562-1755.
    They have storytimes for children Wednesdays at 10:30
    A.M., Fridays at 7:30 P.M., and Saturdays at 11:30 A.M.

Miscellaneous Story Times

In addition to public libraries and commercial establishments, some of San Diego's non-profit and governmental organizations also offer story times. In the summer, many of San Diego's **Parks and Recreation Departments** have evening programs for families that include stories. Call your local city's Parks and Recreation Department for details.

The **San Diego Museum of Art** in Balboa Park offers storytelling on the second Saturday of each month. There is an admission fee; call 619-232-7931 for details.

ADVENTURES IN THE ARTS

Theater

Children in San Diego County have a rich world of theater available to them, whether they want to be spectators of productions geared to young audiences, or whether they want to try their hands as participants in the theater arts. The entries in the following listings all offer opportunities for enjoying theater from either side of the curtain. Interested families can call for details.

☆ San Diego

- San Diego Junior Theater
  Casa del Prado, Balboa Park; 619-239-1311 (Box Office—
  619-239-8355).

- Southeastern Community
  Theater
  5160 Federal Boulevard;
  619-263-7911.

- The J Company
  4126 Executive Drive, La Jolla;
  858-457-3030.

- Christian Youth Theater
  619-588-0206 or 1-800-696-1929
  or www.cctcyt.org.

Note: Despite its name, the Christian Youth Theater is non-denominational and is open to anyone. It is a community-sponsored non-profit organization, so fees are kept lower than at private drama classes.

☆ North County Coastal

- Moonlight Amphitheater Youth Program
  1200 Vale Terrace, Vista; 760-726-1340, ext. 1524.

- North Coast Repertory Theater
  987 Lomas Santa Fe Drive, Solana Beach; 858-481-1055.

- San Diego Actors Theater
  (This group presents family-oriented productions in the Garden Amphitheater of the Inn L'Auberge Del Mar Resort on every other Saturday morning; they also offer theater workshops for children at the same location.)
  1540 Camino Del Mar, Del Mar; 858-268-4494.

- Broadway Bound Youth Theater
  Headquarters in Poway (see below) but also operating in North County Coastal; 858-748-4184.

- Christian Youth Theater
  619-588-0206 or 1-800-696-1929 or www.cctcyt.org.
  Headquarters in El Cajon (see below) but also operating county-wide. See entry above under "San Diego"

Check out the Kids-Go-Free coupons offered from time to time by the San Diego Performing Arts League. Call them at 619-238-0700 or visit their website at www.sandiegoperforms.com.

☆ North County Inland

- California Center for the Arts
  340 N. Escondido Boulevard, Escondido; 760-839-4115,
  www.artcenter.org.

- Patio Playhouse
  201 E. Grand Ave. Suite B, Escondido; 760-746-6669.

- Poway Center for the Performing Arts
  15498 Espola Road, Poway; 858-748-0505.

- Broadway Bound Youth Theater Foundation
  12636—B10 Poway Road, Poway; 858-748-4184.

- Christian Youth Theater
  619-588-0206 or 1-800-696-1929 or www.cctcyt.org.
  See entry above under "San Diego." This organization
  operates county-wide.

☆ East County

- Christian Youth Theater
  1545 Pioneer Way, El Cajon 619-588-0206 or
  1-800-696-1929 or www.cctcyt.org.
  See entry above under "San Diego." This organization
  operates county-wide.

- El Cajon Youth Summer Stock (for teens, summer only)
  619-440-3237.

☆ South County

- Lamb's Players Theater
  1142 Orange Ave. Coronado; 619-437-0600.

- Christian Youth Theater
  1-619-588-0206 or 1-800-696-1929 or www.cctcyt.org.
  See entry above under "San Diego." This organization
  operates county-wide.

- San Diego Junior Theater
  3rd and Davidson Ave., Chula Vista; 619-239-1311 or
  www.juniortheater.org.

Music

As is true in the case of theater, the world of music is available to San Diego children from both sides—that of spectator and that of participant. The listings below do not include the countless sources of private music lessons available to children; those are listed in telephone directories and are advertised in publications for families, such as *San Diego Family* and *San Diego Parent*. For inexpensive music lessons, check with your local Department of Parks and Recreation or your local school. Commercial businesses where musical instruments are sold often provide instruction, as well.

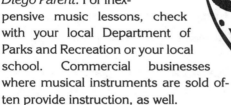

- San Diego Children's Choir; 760-632-5467.
- San Diego Symphony's Kids Concerts; 619-235-0804.
- San Diego Chamber Orchestra's Carnival Classics; 858-350-0290 or 1-888-848-7326, www.sdco.org.
- San Diego Civic Youth Orchestra; 858-484-9635, www.sandiegocyo.org.
- San Diego Youth Symphony; 619-233-3232.
- Starlight Musical Theater (offers family-friendly programs); 619-544-7827 or www.starlighttheatre.org.
- San Dieguito Performing Arts Association; 760-752-5078.
- San Diego Youth Master Chorale; 619-685-7701.
  (**Note:** Many of this organization's productions are **free** to the audience—a truly worthwhile family outing!)
- La Jolla Chamber Music Society's Family Concerts; 858-459-3728.
- **Note** free pipe organ concerts in Balboa Park during the summer each Sunday at 2:00 P.M. Call 619-702-8138 or visit www.serve.com/sosorgan.

Circus Arts

Did you ever dream of running away to join the circus? Well, here are two programs that give your child the skills—not to run away, but to be a real circus performer!

☆ Fern Street Circus (San Diego)

> **Golden Hills Recreation Center, 2600 Golf Course Drive, San Diego; 619-235-9756.**
>
> Fern Street Community Arts, Inc. sponsors a **free** After-School Circus Skills Program for children age 6 years and up (juggling, tumbling, aerial, clowning, and specialty acts.)

Fern Street's program is designed to be a series of on-going classes, not an afternoon crash course in Circus Arts!

☆ Trapeze High (North County Coastal)

> **1466 N. Coast Hwy, Leucadia; 619-269-0657; www. trapezehigh.com.**
>
> A training facility where people of all ages, abilities, and skill levels can experience the thrill of circus-style flying trapeze. They take kids of any age, and their prices vary depending on what your kids want to do.

Visual Arts

Check with your local Parks and Recreation Department and your local library for arts and crafts classes for kids. Some of the community's non-profit organizations, such as the California Center for the Arts in Escondido (760-738-4138), offer art classes at rates lower than are found in the private sector. A few of the major resources for children interested in art enrichment are listed below.

- The **San Diego Art Institute** features a Young Artists Gallery that highlights work from students in the San Diego region. You will find the Institute in the House of Charm in Balboa Park, 619-236-0011. Hours are Tuesday through Saturday from 10:00 A.M. to 4:00 P.M.; Sunday noon to 4:00 P.M. Children under 12 are always admitted free; adults pay $3 except on the third Tuesday of each month, when admission is free for all.

- The **Museum of Contemporary Art** has a branch in La Jolla and a branch in San Diego; the former is at 700 Prospect St, 858-454-3541 and the latter is at 1001 Kettner Blvd. at Broadway, 619-234-1001. On the first Sunday of each month, **free programs tailored for kids** between the ages of 5 and 12 are available at both locations. Admission to the museum is free for all on the first Sunday and the third Tuesday of each month.

- The **San Diego Museum of Art** in Balboa Park offers **Sunday Family Days** throughout the year. During the summer months, classes are available for children. Call 619-232-7931.

- **Art Tours, Inc.** at 5616 La Jolla Boulevard in La Jolla offers both art instruction for kids and art tours for kids, designed to kindle interest and excitement over fine art in the everyday environment. They also offer an after-school enrichment program in various locations. Call 858-459-5922 or visit their website at www.arttoursinc.com.

- **The Athenaeum School of the Arts**, a non-profit institution at 1008 Wall St in La Jolla, offers drawing and painting instruction for children 6 years to 14 years. Call 858-454-5872.

Crafts

Children love to create things that they or their families can use; many a parent or grandparent still treasures the slightly crooked paperweight or the never-used ashtray created by long-ago childish hands. There are a number of opportunities available for kids who want to hone their handicraft skills.

- **Ceramics:** There are several ceramic studios in the county where children can create their own fantasies out of clay. They include (but are not limited to) *Ceramic Art* on Clairemont Mesa Boulevard in San Diego at 858-279-4434; *Claytime Ceramics* on Bacon Street in San Diego at 619-223-6050; *Baubles Etc.* in El Cajon at 619-448-2422; *CeramiCafe* in Del Mar Heights Shopping Center at 858-259-9958 and Grossmont Center at 619-466-4800;

Clay 'n' Latte at two locations: Carmel Mountain at 858-487-9293 and Chula Vista at 619-482-4458.

Note that most of these establishments all allow for drop-in-and-create spontaneity as well as for scheduled instruction.

- **Home Depot** offers one of the best deals in town: free classes for children on how-to-build almost anything. Check with your local branch. **Michael's** craft stores also offer child-oriented classes; theirs are not free, but are very low cost. **Ace Hardware** also sponsors a program known as "Ace Kids." Call them at 1-888-827-4223 for details.

You need to leave your creations at the ceramics studios for a few days so that they can be glazed properly. Prepare your child ahead of time so that there are no melt-downs when you leave empty handed.

- The Chula Vista Nature Interpretive Center offers **Nature Crafts** every Saturday and Sunday from 1:00 to 2:00 for children ages 5 years and up. The cost is 50 cents for the materials used, as well as the admission fee of $1.00 for kids age 6 and over, $3.50 for adults. Call 619-409-5900.

Dance

As with music lessons, private dance lessons abound in most communities, covering all ages and all interests. Several **YMCAs** provide dance lessons, as well, and—as always—your local **Parks and Recreation Department** is a wonderful resource. The **Centro Cultural de la Raza** in Balboa Park offers *ballet folklórico* dance classes (619-235-6135.) The **WorldBeat Center** in Balboa Park offers African dance classes (619-230-1190), as does an organization called Passage Foundation for Children (619-239-7677). For a special treat, watch the newspaper for the coming of "The Nutcracker Suite" ballet, which is performed professionally in San Diego County every year around Christmas time. It's such fun that your children won't even realize they're "getting cultured"! Disney-on-Ice is another spectator dance experience that's well worth a family trip; the show usually visits San Diego in the autumn.

For families who enjoy Country Western music and dancing, a trip to the Big Stone Lodge at 12237 Old Pomerado Road in Poway (858-748-1617) is worth while. On Sunday afternoons, they offer family specials that include food and dancing for the whole family.

Journalism

The *San Diego Union Tribune* offers an opportunity to young critics between the ages of 6 and 17 to review plays, movies, books, or any other family-oriented event. Reviews that are chosen are published on Saturdays along with the reviewer's photograph. Check the "Family" section of the *Union Tribune*'s Saturday edition for details.

Adventures in the Sciences

☆ Reuben H. Fleet Space Theater and Science Center Planetarium (San Diego)

Balboa Park; 619-238-1233.

Details of this marvelously interactive science center are listed in Chapter 2. As a pure adventure in science, a visit here can't be beat. On the first Wednesday of each month, at 7:00 P.M., the famous IMAX theater turns into a planetarium and the resident astronomer presents a program called "Through the Telescope," pointing out celestial features that families can identify from their own backyard. Following this program, volunteer amateur astronomers from San Diego's Astronomy Association set up their telescopes behind the Science Center and invite everyone to take a look. **Admission** to the "Through the Telescope" show is $5 for adults, $3 for children. (Admission price includes admission to the center's exhibits.) Call the above number to confirm times, dates, and prices.

You don't have to attend the show at the Ruben H. Fleet Science Center to enjoy the free informal program offered by the Astronomy Association!

Palomar Observatory

☆ Palomar Observatory (North County Inland)

Highway of Stars on Palomar Mountain off Highway 76; 760-742-2119.
   Open daily from 9:00 A.M. to 4:00 P.M.
   Admission: free.

Operated by the California Institute of Technology, the Palomar Observatory sits at 5500 feet atop Mt. Palomar and houses one of the world's largest telescopes. Visitors cannot actually look through the telescope (even the astronomers who work here don't actually look through it!); but you can view it from a special viewing room, and you can visit the museum where wonderful illuminated photos of planets and galaxies entertain young astronauts. A visit to the observatory makes a great "companion" field

128

trip to a visit to the Reuben Fleet Space Theater in Balboa Park (see below and Chapter 2). Palomar Mountain offers fine picnicking and hiking, or family camping, so plan a day or weekend outing around a trip to the Observatory.

☆ Star Parties (East County)

From time to time throughout the year, when conditions are favorable, members of the San Diego Astronomy Association bring their telescopes (many of them homemade) to a special location where celestial viewing is excellent. There they offer the public a chance for star viewing and astronomy chit-chat. These star parties are free, and they make an unforgettable family outing for those who enjoy peering into the universe. For information on the next star party, call the San Diego Astronomy Association at 619-645-8940, or visit their website at www.sdaa.org.

☆ Other Stargazing Opportunities

Palomar College (North County Inland) in San Marcos opens its planetarium to the public on the first three Friday evenings of each month at 7:00 P.M. **Admission** is $3 for adults, $2 for children. These events fill up quickly, and advanced reservations are recommended. Call 760-744-1150, extension 2833 or 2516 for reservations and more information. The **Mount Laguna** telescope **(East County)** is available for public stargazing on Friday and Saturday evenings during the summer months. **Admission** is free, but reservations must be made at the Cleveland National Forest Ranger Station near the Laguna Forest Campground. (See Appendix 1.) Call 619-594-6182 for further information.

Classes for Kids

During the summer and other school holidays there is a veritable banquet of classes available to kids; many of the resources described below also provide weekend classes throughout the school year. Even better, many of them allow grown-up kids to participate, too! For any that fit your or your children's interests, call for more detailed information.

☆ Stephen Birch Aquarium

2300 Expedition Way, La Jolla; 858-534-3474 or www.aquarium.ucsd.edu.

Classes for grades K through 12 on marine life, including tidepooling and snorkeling excursions.

☆ Chula Vista Nature Interpretive Center

1000 Gunpowder Point Drive, Chula Vista; 619-409-5900 or www.chulavistanaturecenter.org.

Classes for pre-school aged children to teens on the ecology of the intertidal salt marsh, marine life, and environmental awareness. Lots of "hands on" experience.

☆ Helen Woodward Animal Center

6461 El Apajo Rd., Fairbanks Ranch; 858-756-4117 or www.animalcenter.org.

There are parent participation classes for tots between the ages of 2 years and 4 years called "First Friends." During the summer, professional storytellers offer "Animal Tales at Twilight"—families can bring a picnic supper and listen to tall tales and true about our furry, feathered, and scaly friends. For real animal lovers, there are opportunities to volunteer caring for orphaned animals at the Center.

☆ San Diego Zoo

San Diego; 619-234-3153 or www.sandiegozoo.org; and

San Diego Wild Animal Park

Escondido; 760-747-8702 or www.sandiegozoo.org/wap.

Meet the animals up close and personal, and learn some of their secrets in the year-round classes offered for kids, and for kids and adults together. **Overnight experiences** for older children are offered during the summer months.

☆ SeaWorld

San Diego; 619-226-3901 or www.seaworld.com.

Classes for families and for children from age 3 up. During the summer, SeaWorld offers Camp Sea World for preschoolers through high school seniors. The camps for little ones ages 3 and 4 include parent involvement and run just a few hours in the morning. Older children can extend their hours and can even bring sleeping bags for **nighttime Sea World adventures**. Prices vary. For information on Camp Sea World, call 619-226-3903.

☆ San Diego Natural History Museum

Balboa Park, 619-232-3821 (education department is extension 203) or www.sdnhm.org.

There are educational programs for all ages, throughout the year. A perennial favorite is Ms. Frizzle and her magic school bus; she is a regular at the Natural History Museum on Sundays and often appears at other times (sometimes even at other places)! They will be happy to send you a catalogue of upcoming classes, programs, field trips, and other adventures.

☆ San Diego Museum of Man

Balboa Park, 619-239-2001 or www.museumofman.org.

Preschool through 12th Grade. Learn how to be a bone detective; explore mummies and the mysteries of Egypt; discover Indian drama and games. Year 'round classes, and extended summer programs. Call for a brochure.

☆ Reuben H. Fleet Space Theater and Science Center

Balboa Park, 619-238-1233 or www.rhfleet.org.

Grades K through 9—workshops in science; space adventures. You can learn about the human body, journey through the galaxy, experiment with computer science, and lots more in the interactive programs offered here. Classes throughout the year.

☆ The Elementary Institute of Science

588 Euclid Avenue, San Diego (temporary residence as of press time, while new state-of-the-art center is being built); 619-263-2302. E-mail eisca@aol.com.

This non-profit, community-supported institute provides kids with hands-on experiences designed to stimulate appreciation and understanding of science and technology. Their classes are targeted at children between 7 and 13 years of age, and cover biology, chemistry, computer science, photography, engineering, and physical science. They offer after-school, weekend, and summer hours. The summer program costs $40 per week; this price includes lunch, a snack, a T-shirt and a field trip. Their after-school and Saturday programs are $20 a month. Call or e-mail for more information.

☆ The San Diego Humane Society

619--299-7012; 887 Sherman St. at Morena Boulevard.

During the summer, children between the ages of 9 and 11 can learn how to care for animals in the Humane Society's week-long day camps. Call for more information.

CHAPTER 9

Adventures of the Body

We like to believe that most of the adventures described throughout this book can be fun for children of any age, depending on individual tastes and on the good judgement of parents. But there's no getting away from the fact that older children—pre-teens and adolescents in particular—can sometimes be a challenge to those who seek to entertain them in a safe and family-friendly manner. This chapter, in which we explore both participatory sports and spectator sports, may be particularly helpful to families with those hard-to-please older kids.

Besides, exercising together is great for the physical and emotional health of any family; and San Diego, with its delightful year-round climate, is an ideal place in which to enjoy a host of outdoor activities. So pick your favorite sport, or try a new one; take the family, and get moving!

☆ Roller Blading

There are a number of excellent areas in the county for family skating. One of the best is Mission Bay Park (see Chapter 3) with its miles and miles of wide, paved sidewalks. In Coronado, the path that starts at the ferry landing (just off First Street, two blocks east of Orange Avenue) is another great skate place. Many of San Diego's bike paths are also good for skating, and are safe from traffic. For a free map of our local bike trails, call 619-231-BIKE.

Note that skating is prohibited in Balboa Park and is strongly discouraged throughout the city of Del Mar.

The following San Diego County roller rinks all have special family times, and also offer lessons for kids. Of course,

they will rent you a pair of skates if
you don't own any. Call for days,
times, and admission prices.

- Rollerskateland (South
  County)
  626 L. St. Chula Vista;
  619-420-4761.

- Skate San Diego (South
  County)
  700 E. 24th St., National City;
  619-474-1000,
  www.skatesandiego.com.

- Skate World (San Diego)
  6907 Linda Vista Road, San
  Diego; 858-560-9278 or recorded information at 858-560-9349.

- Ups-N-Downs Roller Rink (North County Inland)
  862 N. Broadway, Escondido; 760-745-5966.

- Escondido Sports Center (North County Inland)
  3315 Bear Valley Parkway, Escondido (in Kit Carson Park);
  760-839-5425; www.ci.escondido.ca.us. Follow the "Arts
  and Entertainment" link to the Escondido Sports Center.
  Note: This center offers **roller hockey.**

- Roller Skating in the Garage (North County Inland)
  San Marcos Community Center; 760-744-9000.
  Note: This is a special program, sponsored by the City of
  San Marcos on selected Friday evenings during the spring
  and summer. There is no admission cost.

- Oceanside Roller Rink (North County Coastal)
  315 Windward Way, Oceanside; 760-722-5554.

- Parkway Sports Center (East County)
  1055 Ballantyne, El Cajon; 619-442-9623.
  Note: This center offers **roller hockey**.

- Rollerskate Land (East County)
  9365 Mission Gorge Rd., Santee; 619-562-3791.

Note: This center offers **roller hockey.** In addition, there is Rollerblade's Blade School, which offers two-hour **classes** on Saturdays at Mission Valley Center for kids 7 years old and up. For more information, call them at 1-800-950-7655 or check their web site at www.bladeschool.com.

☆ Skateboarding

Anyone with a skateboard fan in the family needs to find some relatively safe locations for this popular youth sport. The following is a partial list of the skateboard parks in the county. Almost all the parks require protective gear, including a helmet and elbow pads. Most recommend knee pads as well. Many of the parks will provide protective gear for a deposit or for a small fee. Some of the parks listed below are free, and some charge admission. The admission costs vary with age and, in some cases, with membership. Call the individual park for details.

- Imperial Beach Bored? Skate Park (South County)
  425 Imperial Beach Boulevard, Imperial Beach
  This skatepark is run by the city of Imperial Beach. For details on hours and prices, call the city at 619-423-8300.

- Andy A. Rogers Skate Park (South County)
  635 Seacoast Boulevard, Imperial Beach
  This is one of the county's newest skate parks; check it out!

- South Bay Family YMCA Skate Park (South County)
  1201 Paseo Magda, Chula Vista; 619-421-8805 or
  www.southbay.ymca.org/skatepark.html.
  This park includes a beginner's area. There is a fee; call or visit the website for information.

- Washington Street Skate Park (San Diego)
  Foot of Washington Street in Mission Hills.
  Admission: free.

- Robb Field Skate Park (San Diego)
  2525 Bacon Street, Ocean Beach; 619-525-8486.
  Call for hours and admission cost. This park has a **beginners** area.

- YMCA Krause Family Skate Park (San Diego)
  3401 Clairemont Drive, Clairemont; 619-279-9254.
     Call for hours and admission prices. This park has a special area for **beginners**.

- Narrowgate Skate Park (San Diego)
  5331 Mt. Alifan Drive, Clairemont.
     Check for admission prices and hours at 858-277-4991, ext. 298.

- Escondido Sports Center (North County Inland)
  333 Bear Valley Parkway, Escondido (in Kit Carson Park).
     Check for hours and admission prices at 760-839-5425.

- Magdalena Ecke Family YMCA (North County Coastal)
  200 Saxony Road, Encinitas; 760-942-9622;
  www.ecke.ymca.org.
     Call or check the website for hours and cost. **Beginners** area.

- Carlsbad Safety Center (North County Coastal)
  2560 Orion Way, Carlsbad.
     Admission: free; **Beginners** area.

- Oceanside Skate Park (North County Coastal)
  Northeast corner of Pier Way and Myers Way, Oceanside;
  760-435-5041.
     Admission: free

- Vista Skate Park (North County Coastal)
  635 Alta Vista Drive, Vista (Civic Center Park).
     Admission: free. Call 760-726-1340, ext. 1576 for hours.

- Woodglen Vista Skate Park (East County)
  10250 Woodglen Vista Rd. off north Magnolia, Santee.
     Admission: free. Call 619-258-4100, ext. 222 for hours.

- Kennedy Skate Park (East County)
  1675 E. Madison, El Cajon; 619-441-1676.
     Admission: free

- Borrego Badlands Skate Park (East County)
  630 Cahuilla Rd. Borrego Springs; 760-767-9989, www.
  borregobadlands.org.

Hours vary by season. Please call for information. Annual fee is $30, with no additonal session fee on weekdays; weekend (2-hour) session fee is $5.00.

- Skate Mesa
  East County YMCA, 619-464-1323.
  This skate park includes a combination of concrete and wood skating surfaces.

☆ Ice Skating

Ice skating in southern California? Sure, why not! There are three ice rinks in San Diego County, and all offer **lessons** to kids and parents. Or simply go during family skating times, and try your skill.

- Ice Town, University Town Center (San Diego)
  4545 La Jolla Village Drive, La Jolla; 858-452-9110.
  Admission: $6.50 per person plus $2.50 per person for skate rental.

- San Diego Ice Arena (San Diego)
  11048 Ice Skate Place, San Diego; 858-530-1825.
  Admission: $5.50 per person plus $2.50 for skate rental.

- Iceoplex (North County Inland)
  555 N. Tulip St. Escondido; 760-489-5550.
  Admission: $6.50 for adults, $5.50 for children under 12. Rentals are $2.25 for figure skates, $2.50 for hockey skates.
  Note that the Iceoplex has an **ice hockey** program for youngsters and for adults.

☆ Horseback Riding

There are a number of stables throughout San Diego County that rent horses and/or lead trail rides. Most also offer lessons. Those listed below provide guided trail rides. To simply rent a horse or two for a few hours, consult your local yellow pages under "Horse Rentals" for other stables near you. **Note** that many local stables also offer **lessons**. Children under 6 years old usually are required to ride with an adult; children 6 years and older can usually ride their own horse.

Note that the YMCA runs a resident camp during the summer that specializes in horseback riding. Call 858-292-4034 for details.

- Happy Trails (San Diego)
  12115 Black Mountain Rd., San Diego; 858-271-8777.
  This stable specializes in riding through the Los Peñasquitos Canyon Preserve. Rates start at $20 per hour, and decrease with numbers of hours of rental. An all-day ride includes a barbecue. Call for reservations.

- Bright Valley Farms (East County)
  12310 Campo Road, Spring Valley; 619-670-1861.
  Ride the scenic trails of the Sweetwater River Valley. Trail rides as well as lessons available.

- Sandi's Rental Stable (South County)
  2060 Hollister St., San Diego; 619-424-3124.

All levels of riders are welcomed here, from absolute novices to experts. You can ride the beach for three hours for $40 per person, or you can ride the river trail (along the Tijuana River) for an hour for $20 per person. Reservations are not necessary.

- Sweetwater Farms (South County)
  3051 Equitation Lane, Bonita;
  619-475-3134, www.sweetwaterhorses.com.
  This establishment offers pony rides for kids every weekend. In addition to lessons, they also offer day camps and horse shows. Call for hours and prices.

- Julian Stables Trail Rides (North County Inland)
  760-765-1598.
  For $35 per person, you get a guided trail ride through some of the loveliest back country in San Diego County. Call for reservations.

☆ Bicycling

There are endless wonderful places for families to bicycle in San Diego County. Most of the trails described in Chapter 5 would be great for those with mountain bikes; Chapter 3 describes the joys of bicycling along the boardwalk in **Mission Beach** where many rental shops are available. There are several bicycle rental shops along Fifth Avenue near **Balboa Park**, another fine family bicycling area. **Mission Bay**, with its flat terrain and easy bike paths, is another popular area for families on wheels. In the downtown San Diego area, try the wood-planked **Embarcadero trail** that takes off from 1050 North Harbor Drive.

One of the best bike trails in the North County is the **Camp Pendleton Coast** ride: Take I-5 to Harbor Drive and turn right on San Rafael Drive. You can cruise north along the coast for almost 40 miles along an old 4-lane highway with virtually no traffic. Also, between Carlsbad and Solana Beach the **coast highway** has a designated bike lane, and there are several bike rental shops along the coast highway in that area.

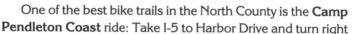

Note: For a free San Diego Regional Cycling map, simply call 619-231-2453.

For a special and unique adventure, consider a guided bicycle tour of **Coronado**. These tours last two hours and have very few hills to climb. They are led by guides from the Hotel del Coronado, and include a touch of old San Diego history as well as the bike rental and helmet. Kids may be a little bored with the history, but the bicycling is easy, and there is always a stop for frozen yogurt. Call 619-435-6611 for rates, dates, and times.

If you'd rather skip the guided tour, you can rent bicycles at the Old Ferry Landing complex on Coronado, or bring your own bikes across on the ferry.

The Magdalena Ecke Family YMCA in Encinitas has recently opened an area dedicated to **dirt bikes**, where kids can practice their stunts in safety. It's called **Dirt Bike Haven** and is located at 200 Saxony Road in Encinitas. For more information, call the YMCA at 760-942-9622 or check their website at www.ecke.ymca.org.

☆ Bowling

Most bowling alleys have a junior bowl time and/or a family bowl time. Some also offer "Cosmic Bowling" which is a hit with the **pre-teen and teen crowd,** as it involves popular music and a light show. Call your local bowling alley for details.

☆ Laser Tag

For a fun and different kind of kids birthday party, check with your local bowling alley. Most will rent to groups.

Here's a high-tech sport for twenty-first century families! It's an interactive game in which the players take a laser-pulse phaser into the play area and try to "tag" opponents. The following is a partial list of centers offering this new activity.

- Laser Storm (East County)
    9365 Mission Gorge Rd., Santee; 619-562-3791.
        Cost is $3.50 for the first ten-minute game and $2.50 for each subsequent ten-minute game. Call for hours. Children must be at least 3 years old to play.

- Ultrazone (San Diego)
    3146 Sports Arena Blvd., Ste 21, San Diego; 619-221-0100.
        Cost is $6.50 for a fifteen-minute game. Call for hours. Children must be at least 7 years old to play.

- Poway Entertainment Center (North County Inland)
    12941 Poway Rd., Poway; 858-748-9110.
        Call for specific hours and prices. No age limit, but child must be big enough to wear the vest.

☆ Paintball

This is another new game for those looking for something different. It's a little like the old "capture the flag" game, except you eliminate your opponents with bright blobs of paint! Best for **kids 10 years and older.**

- Borderland Paintball Park (East County)
  13531 Otay Lakes Rd., Jamul; 858-536-4257.
     Open weekends only, 9:00 A.M. to 4:30 P.M. No children under 10. **Admission** is $15 for those over the age of 15 and $8 for kids ages 10 through 15. Equipment rental is $20.

- Hidden Valley Paintball Park (North County Inland)
  25320 Lake Wohlford Rd., Escondido; 760-737-8870.
     Open weekends only, 8:00 A.M. to 4:00 P.M. **Admission** is $15 for a full day, $10 for a half day.

WATER SPORTS

☆ Boating

You can learn to kayak, to canoe, or to sail; you can simply explore a lake on a little paddle boat or a rowboat. The establishments listed below will rent you equipment and will also provide lessons if needed. Call for rates. Also **note** that most of

the **lakes** discussed in Chapter 4 will rent rowboats and/or paddle boats.

- Aqua Adventures Kayak School (San Diego)
  1548 Quivira Way, San Diego; 619-523-9577 or www.aqua-adventures.com.
- Windsport (San Diego)
  844 W. Mission Bay Drive, San Diego; 858-488-4642.
     This shop rents **windsurfing** equipment as well as kayaks
- Resort Watersports (San Diego)
  Catamaran Hotel
  3999 Mission Blvd, Pacific Beach; 858-539-8696.

- Bahia Hotel
  998 W. Mission Bay Dr., Mission Beach; 858-488-0551.
  The Catamaran and Bahia shops rent **sailboats** as well as kayaks.

- Mission Bay Sportscenter (San Diego)
  1010 Santa Clara Place; 858-488-1004.
  This shop rents **sailboats** as well as kayaks, and offers a seasonal **water sports camp for kids.**

- CP Watersports (San Diego)
  San Diego Hilton Hotel, 1775 East Mission Bay Drive; 619-275-8945.
  This shop rents **canoes and windsurfers** as well as kayaks.

- California Water Sports Rentals (North County Coastal)
  4215 Harrison St., Carlsbad (Snug Harbor Marina); 760-434-3089.
  This shop rents **canoes** as well as kayaks.

- Carlsbad Paddle Sports (North County Coastal)
  2780 Carlsbad Blvd., Carlsbad; 760-434-8686.
  This shop specializes in kayaks and **leads kayak trips.**

☆ Fishing

In Chapters 3 and 4, we detailed some of the best fishing spots in the county for kids and families. There are a couple of great opportunities for getting some expert **instruction** on fishing, for those who want a little help getting started.

Every Saturday morning at 10:00, the supervising ranger at Lake Cuyamaca offers **free fishing classes.** Contact the ranger at 619-447-8123.

If **fly fishing** is what attracts you, contact the San Diego Fly Fishers regarding their Sunday morning lessons at Lake Murray. (San Diego Fly Fishers can be contacted through Stroud's Tackle at 619-276-4822.)

For young fisherman and their families, a **deep sea fishing** trip can be the adventure of a lifetime, and will provide lots of dinner-table yarns about the one that got away. The ocean fishing boats listed below offer fishing trips ranging in length from half a day to several days. Fishing poles are available for rent if you don't have your own; food and beverages can be purchased on board. Prices will vary with the length of the trip you desire and the number of people in your party; most offer discounts for children. Anyone over the age of sixteen needs a fishing license; a day license can be purchased at the dock. Call for details at the phone numbers listed below; remember that, especially during the summer, these trips fill up quickly, so plan to make reservations ahead of time.

- Helgren's
315 Harbor Drive South,
Oceanside; 760-722-2133,
www.helgrensportfishing.com.

The Coast Guard requires that every passenger on these boats weighs at least 35 pounds! Leave the small fry at home.

- Islandia Sportfishing
1551 W. Mission Bay Drive, San Diego; 619-222-1164,
www.islandiasport.com.

- Seaforth Sportfishing
1717 Quivera Road, San Diego;. 619-224-3383 (information and reservations), 619-224-6695 (fishing report).

- H&M Sportfishing Landing
2803 Emerson St., San Diego; 619-222-1144,
www.hmlanding.com.

- Fisherman's Landing
2838 Garrison St., San Diego; 619-221-8500,
www.fishermanslanding.com.

- Point Loma Sportsfishing
1403 Scott St., San Diego; 619-223-1627,
www.pointlomasportfishing.com.

- Captain Ward Lindsay
2803 Emerson St., San Diego; 619-523-0520.

☆ Swimming

Call your local YMCA or your local Department of Parks and Recreation for swim lessons for kids of all ages, usually starting at about 6 months of age. The city of San Diego offers a

Swim Hot Line to help families find the nearest aquatics program. Call them at 619-685-1322.

There are also many private sources of swim lessons that you will find advertised in the yellow pages of the phone book, and in local family-oriented publications such as *San Diego Family* and *San Diego Parent* (both available free at public libraries and at many business establishments.) There are many municipal swimming pools that are available to local residents for extremely low rates. We mention two of them here for their special attractions, but check with your own community (usually through your local Department of Parks and Recreation) for the municipal pool nearest you. Most have family swim times and/or lessons.

- The Plunge (San Diego)
  3115 Ocean Front Walk in Mission Beach; 858-488-3110.
      This is San Diego's **largest indoor swimming pool**, and it is kept at a temperature of 84 degrees all year. There's a roped shallow end where parents with kids can keep separated from the lap swimmers. **Admission** is $2.50 for adults and $2.00 for children. **Note**: The Plunge is available for swimming only at certain hours. Call the above phone number for details.

- Las Posas Aquatic Center (North County Inland)
  111 Richmar, San Marcos; 760-744-9000.
      There is an access ramp to this pool **for disabled individuals**. Kids love the "sprayground" area on the deck by the pool. **Admission** is $2.00 per person. Call for hours.

☆ Surfing

The YMCA runs a **Surfing Camp** during the summer for kids ages 7 to 16 where youngsters learn surfing skills and ocean safety. Call 858-292-4034. The Mission Bay Sportcenter, listed above, also offers **surfing lessons**. Call 858-488-1004.

You're never too young to enjoy a surfboard!

photo by Bunny Smith

During the summer, budding surfers can practice their skills at The Wave Waterpark in Vista or at The Wave attraction in Belmont Park (see Chapter 10 for details on both.)

The Wave attractions both have height requirements; check them out before making any promises to your kids! The one at Belmont Park allows both body surfing and board surfing. If you have a young body surfer, he or she needs to be wary of wayward boards.

☆ Junior Lifeguard Programs

The city of San Diego offers training during the summer for children between the ages of 9 years and 17 years who want to learn the skills of a lifeguard. Although there is a substantial cost for this program, **scholarships** are available. North County youth can join the junior lifeguard program in Solana Beach. Call 858-581-7861 or see www.sandiego.gov/lifeguards/junior.

☆ San Diego Parasail Adventures

1641 Quivira Rd. (Seaforth Boat Rental Building) 619-223-4386.

At $49 per person per hour, this is not an inexpensive adventure! However, it is spectacular to see San Diego from 300 feet up. Tandem rides are offered, so kids can fly with a parent or older sibling. Reservations are strongly recommended.

> *The minimum weight requirement to fly alone is 70 pounds. Children under this requirement can fly with an adult.*

TEAM SPORTS

> *Virtually all Boomers have batting cages. There is also an indoor batting facility called Batters Box in Poway at 12576 Kirkham Court. In addition to batting practice, they offer hitting and pitching lessons on a drop-in basis (minimum 15 minutes). Call 1-877-U-CAN-BAT for more information.*

For your local **Little League** club, check your telephone directory's yellow pages under "Baseball Clubs," or check the business section (the pink-bordered pages) of the Pacific Bell's white pages. (Look under the heading of your city; for example, "Oceanside National Little League.") Of course, you can always check out the regional website at www.littleleague.org where you can click on "league finder" to locate the club nearest you. The telephone number for the national headquarters is 909-887-6444.

There are also a number of commercial **baseball schools** in our community. A few of them are listed below, but there are many others; check your phone book's yellow pages under Baseball Schools.

- San Diego Padres Camp for Kids; 1-800-336-CAMP (2267).

- Allstar Baseball (offers year-round baseball camps) 858-792-4025.

- Valley Baseball School and Softball Academy; 858-792-2255.

- Randy Jones Baseball Academy; 619-744-8799.

- Baseball Academy of San Diego State University 619-594-4186.

Many communities offer **girls' softball leagues**. Check Pacific Bell's White Pages directory under the pink-bordered business section, and look for your city (for example, "Vista Girls' Softball Association").

For your local **youth soccer league**, check your telephone directory's yellow pages under "Soccer Clubs" or visit the website of the American Youth Soccer Association at www.soccer.org.

Pop Warner football (www.popwarner.com) is a program to teach young children the basics of the game. There are several Pop Warner groups in the county. A few are listed below. **Note** that the Pop Warner organization also offers **cheerleading** training for kids; they are an integral part of every game.

- Grossmont/La Mesa; 619-464-3736.
- El Cajon; 619-464-8312.
- San Diego; 619-423-8597.
- Balboa (San Diego); 619-262-3731.
- Escondido; 760-743-4219.
- Palomar (serving North County); 760-729-4502.
- Rancho Bernardo; 619-748-6104.
- San Marcos; 760-591-5009.

In addition, several cities offer **flag football** for youngsters through their Departments of Recreation. Check your own city in the Government pages (blue-bordered) of the white pages phone directory.

INDIVIDUAL SPORTS

☆ Tennis

Many YMCAs and Parks and Recreation Departments offer tennis lessons for kids. An organization called Youth Tennis San Diego, at 4490 West Point Loma Boulevard, is a community-sponsored non-profit organization dedicated to teaching tennis skills to all youngsters. Fees are lower than for private lessons, and scholarships are available. Call 619-221-9000 for more information.

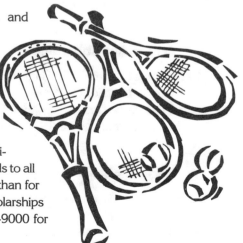

☆ Gymnastics and Tumbling

Virtually every YMCA and every Parks and Recreation Department offers classes, starting with pre-schoolers; there are also many private sources advertised in the yellow pages of the phone book under "Gymnastics Instruction."

☆ Martial Arts

As with gymnastics, lessons in karate and other martial arts are available to children through most branches of the YMCA, most Departments of Recreation, and many private teachers. It's a great way to learn self-confidence and discipline! You can also check out the yellow pages under "Martial Arts."

☆ Golf

For a truly awesome website covering all kinds of youth sports, check out www.youth sports.com/ showme. html.

For children who want to learn to play golf, one of the best resources in the county is the **ProKids Golf Academy and Learning Center** located in the Colina Park/College area of San Diego. They are a community sponsored non-profit organization, so they can keep their fees down and can offer **scholarships** to kids who need them. For details, call 619-582-7884 or see www.prokidsgolf.com.

There is also a **Junior Golf Association** in town; call 619-280-8505.

☆ Ski and Snowboarding

Leave it to southern California to offer snow-free ski and snowboard lessons! Check out the Adventure Ski and Snowboard School 1105 S. Coast Highway in Encinitas (inside Hansen's shop). The phone number is 760-942-2188. These lessons are appropriate for all ages and abilities.

☆ Rock Climbing

Rock climbing is growing in popularity; it's a great way for youngsters to gain strength and confidence. The following organizations have indoor climbing walls and offer instruction.

- Solid Rock Gym
    2074 Hancock St., San Diego; 619-299-1124.
    13026 Stowe Drive, Poway; 858-748-9011.
    992 Rancheros Drive, San Marcos; 619-299-1124.
    www.solidrockgym.com.
        Day passes are $10; after 5:00 and on weekends, day
    passes are $12 for adults, $10 for children 16 and younger.

- Vertical Hold Climbing Center
    9580 Distribution Ave. San Diego; 858-586-7572 or
    www.verticalhold.com.
        Day passes are $12 for everyone.

- UCSD Recreation
    9500 Gilman Drive, La Jolla; 858-534-4037.
        Fully supervised indoor climbing instruction for kids 5
    years and up. They offer 4-week Saturday courses for about
    $23 per person.

- Santa Margarita Family YMCA
    1965 Peacock Boulevard, Oceanside; 760-758-0808.
    Classes for children from the age of 6 years. Fees vary, de-
    pending upon whether you're a YMCA member or not, and
    the extent to which you wish to be involved.

☆ Running

The San Diego Marathon, an annual event usually taking place
in January, includes a children's one-mile race for kids between
the ages of 7 and 12 years. There's also a half-mile run for 5- and
6-year olds, a quarter-mile run for 3- and 4-year olds, and a
25-yard dash for the under-3 crowd. Children's runs are all
non-competitive; the emphasis
is on fun. For information, call
858-792-2900.

Additionally, check out
the Junior Carlsbad Run, usually held in March. This
event is for kids only,
from age 12 on down to
the diaper set. There is an

entry fee. Call 858-450-6510 or visit the website at www.eliteracing.com for details.

In May, look for Dr. Seuss Kids Magic Mile Run/Walk in San Diego. Call 858-792-2900 or visit www.ut-drseuss8k.com.

SPECTATOR SPORTS

Do spectator sports really count as "adventures of the body?" Maybe if you cheer hard enough, you'll work up a sweat! In any case, taking the family to a ball game is a time-honored way to spend a fun few hours together, if you and your kids are sports fans. Below, we've listed some of the better-known spectator sports in town. But don't forget that an outing with the family to watch your local high school team play football can be just as much fun, and a lot less expensive, than professional sporting events.

San Diego's major sports stadium (as of press time) is **Qualcomm Stadium** in Mission Valley. You can call them at 619-641-3131 and they'll be happy to send you a list of up-coming events.

The teams that get the most attention in our community are the **San Diego Chargers** football team and the **San Diego Padres** baseball team. Don't forget that the **San Diego State University's football team** plays at Qualcomm Stadium too, and their ticket prices are significantly lower than are those of the Chargers. Call 619-283-7378 for details on college games. Remember, when you are budgeting for an outing to Qualcomm Stadium, that **parking** is $6 per car for Padres and Chargers games and $5 per car for San Diego State games. Bus service and trolley service to the stadium is convenient and affordable; check it out!

☆ San Diego Chargers

Call 877-CHARGERS for ticket information, or visit the website at www.chargers.com.

The Chargers training camp has moved to Los Angeles. However, they still have a mini-training camp right after the NFL season at their training facility on the campus of UCSD. Fans can go there to get autgraphs and see the players up close. Call 858-874-4500 for information.

The San Diego Chargers have a top-notch cheerleading squad, and they offer a **"Junior Charger Girl"** Program for kids between the ages of 6 and 16. Interested girls will work with the professional cheerleaders and will perform at one of the games. Call the Chargers' Public Relations department at 858-874-4500 for further details.

If you plan to attend a Charger game with little ones, avoid the rowdy end zones and sit in the upper decks. I also advise avoiding the Oakland game altogether; that particular game gets extremely rowdy!

☆ San Diego Padres

Call 619-280-4636 for ticket information, or visit the website at www.padres.com. Ask about the **Jr. Padres Club** for kids, and about **family ticket packages**.

☆ Soccer and Hockey

In addition to professional football and baseball, San Diego has a professional ice hockey team and an A-league soccer team (only one level below major league). The **San Diego Gulls** play hockey at the Sports Arena between October and March; call 619-224-4625 for ticket information, or visit their website at www.sandiegogulls.com.

During the same season, the hot new women's soccer team, the **San Diego Spirit**, plays at USD's Torero stadium. Call 877-4SOCCER or visit www.sandiegospirit.com.

☆ Arena Football

The San Diego Riptide play all their home games at the San Diego Sports Arena. For information, contact 858-404-0232, 866-RIPTIDE, or www.sandiegoriptide.com.

☆ Ice Hockey

The San Diego Surf is a Junior Hockey Club for kids younger than 20 years. They play at 555 N. Tulip St., in Escondido. Contact them at 619-972-1456 or www.sdjrsurf.com.

☆ Auto and Boat Racing

Auto racing fans can see the real thing at the El Cajon Speedway between March and October; call 619-448-8900 for prices, dates, and times. **Motocross racing** goes on throughout the year at the Carlsbad Raceway; call 760-727-1171. **Hydroplane and Power Boat Racing** attracts fans to Mission Bay in September for the Thunderboats Unlimited weekend. The event includes nighttime fireworks and entertainment for kids. Call 619-225-9160 for ticket information.

☆ San Diego Polo Club

Even some San Diego natives are unaware of the **San Diego Polo Club** (www.sandiegopolo.com) that holds matches on Sundays from June through September at 14555 El Camino Real in Rancho Santa Fe. Kids' activities are available before the matches start, and admission is a bargain at only $5 per person. Call 619-481-9212. They also offer classes; for information, call 858-481-9217.

☆ Golf and Tennis

San Diego's outstanding climate makes it a natural for some major sports events. Two of the most famous are the **Buick Invitational Golf Tournament** held in February at the Torrey Pines Golf Course in La Jolla and, for tennis, the **Acura Classic** held in August at the La Costa Resort in La Costa. For information and tickets to the golf tournament, call 619-281-4653; for the tennis matches, call 760-438-5683.

SPECIAL SPORTS ADVENTURE
The ARCO U.S. Olympic Training Center

There are only three official Olympic Training Centers in the country, and San Diego has one of them. Free tours of the facility are offered daily, and you can often see athletes practicing for track and field, cycling, archery, and lots of other events. The center is located in Chula Vista at 2800 Olympic Parkway. Call them at 619-482-6222 or 619-656-1500 for information on hours.

CHAPTER 10

Excursions, Amusements, Tours

Like most folks, we San Diegans rarely play tourist in our own community. We get caught up in the daily demands of our busy lives and forget that one of the greatest joys of parenthood is the opportunity to share in the playful nature of children, and to do something just because it's fun!

Some of the attractions listed in this chapter are quite costly; others are free or very low cost. All are adventures for the young at heart, whether they be visitors to San Diego, new residents of the area, or old timers who could use a fresh look at their own back yard.

EXCURSIONS ON THE WATER

☆ Harbor Excursions (San Diego)

A cruise around San Diego's harbor makes a relaxing interlude which kids and grown-ups enjoy equally. The excursion boats all include snack bars where you can chow down as you hear about San Diego's history and view the Navy ships and the downtown skyline. Harbor cruises vary in length from one to two hours; for most kids, the shorter excursions are just about right for their attention span. A one-hour tour costs $12 for adults, $6 for children ages 4 to twelve. A two-hour tour costs $17 for adults, $8.50 for children. Boats leave from the Embarcadero on Harbor Drive at the foot of Broadway.

- San Diego Harbor Excursion
  1050 North Harbor Drive; 619-234-4111, www.sdhe.com.

These excursions are all within the harbor; for that reason, they rarely cause motion sickness (unlike whale-watching cruises and deep-sea fishing excursions that head into open sea.) However, if you are particularly sensitive to motion sickness, consult your doctor for preventive medicine.

- Hornblower Cruises
  1066 North Harbor Drive; 619-686-8715,
  www.hornblower.com.

☆ The Coronado Ferry (San Diego and South County)

One of the signs of a real San Diego old timer is the ability to remember when the only way to get to and from the island of Coronado was by ferry. Since the completion of the beautiful Coronado Bay Bridge in 1970, it's been far more efficient for commuters to drive (except sometimes during rush hour when the water route would still probably be faster!). But the re-instated ferry, now freed from its work-a-day role of transporting commuters, exists solely for enjoyment and is one of San Diego's most delightful family excursions. From the Broadway Pier on Harbor Drive in downtown San Diego, ferry boats depart every hour on the hour from 9:00 A.M. to 9:00 P.M. Sunday through Thursday, and from 9:00 A.M. to 10:00 P.M. on Friday and Saturday. Return voyages from Coronado depart every hour on the half-hour. The ride across the bay takes about 15 minutes and costs $2.00 one way for anyone over 3 years old, and 50 cents extra for each bicycle. The view is spectacular, and the boat ride itself is a treat for everyone.

The Old Ferry Landing, on the Coronado side, is lined with attractive shops, restaurants, and **street entertainers** that all combine to create a festive atmosphere. There's also a small **sandy beach** where kids can play in the quiet waters of the bay. From the Old Ferry Landing, many families enjoy **bicycling** around Coronado (bring your own bikes on the ferry, or rent them at the Old Ferry Landing.) Tickets for the ferry can be purchased at San Diego Harbor Excursions, 1050 N. Harbor Drive (phone 619-234-4111). Reservations are not necessary.

☆ San Diego Water Taxi (San Diego and South County)

If you're interested in a "private tour" of San Diego Bay, you can hop into your own water taxi. For $5 per person, a motorized boat will transport you to all points on the bay, from Shelter and Harbor Islands to Chula Vista. **Hours** of operation are 10:00 A.M. to 10:00 P.M. daily.

☆ The Gondola Company (South County)

No, it's not exactly Venice, but you can take a ride around San Diego Bay in an authentic gondola. Whether or not the gondolier includes a serenade is up to you! The gondolas operate out of Loews Coronado Bay Resort at 4000 Coronado Bay Rd. Call 619-424-4000.

AMUSEMENTS IN THE WATER
(Water Parks)

☆ Knott's Soak City USA (South County)

619-661-7373; www.knotts.com/soakcity.sd. 2052 Entertainment Circle, Chula Vista. From I-805, exit Main Street in Chula Vista; drive east and turn right on Entertainment Circle.

Open 10:00 A.M. to 7:00 P.M. daily June through September; weekends only in May, September, and early October.

Admission is $13.95 for children ages 3 to 11, $19.95 for anyone age 12 and up. Note that the price of admission includes free use of plastic inner tubes for any and all rides, and free use of life jackets (required for small children.) Price of admission does not include parking ($4) or locker rental ($4, $6, or $8 depending on the size locker you need.) Season passes are available, and coupons for admission discounts are available at Food-4-Less stores and in local family-oriented publications such as "San Diego Family" and "San Diego Parent."

The food is not very good, and it's overpriced. The lines at the food stands move very slowly. Either consider leaving the park before lunch, coming after lunch, or getting in line early enough so that your kids won't fall apart from hunger!

Of the three water parks in San Diego County, Knott's is the biggest and the most expensive, with 22 different attractions. They include 17 high-speed slides, a large shallow pool in which artificial ocean-like swells are periodically created, a gentle "river" ride, and a few small, low-speed slides for very young children. No food or drink is permitted in the park; there are a few snack bars available. The safety features are outstanding,

Although the park provides shade canopies here and there, during peak visitor times, shade is at a premium. Bring along an extra towel to spread under a tree when you need a shady break, or for enjoying your lunch.

with lifeguards everywhere and rules gently but rigorously enforced.

For any water park, don't forget sunscreen, towels, and dry clothes for everyone! Bring a pair of shoes that you can slip on and off with wet feet (rubber or plastic sandals work best.)

Most of the slides have a 48-inch height minimum requirement, and any child under 36 inches is required to wear a life vest at all times in the water.

☆ The Wave Waterpark (North County Coastal)

760-940-9283; www.wave-waterpark.com; 161 Recreation Drive, Vista. From Highway 78, exit Vista Village Drive in Vista. Follow Vista Village Drive around to where it meets Recreation Drive; turn right, and then right again into the parking lot.

Open daily 10:30 A.M. to 5:30 P.M. June through Labor Day; weekends 11:00 A.M. to 5:00 P.M. Memorial Day weekend and first three weekends in September.

Admission is free for children 2 years and under, $6.75 for children under 42 inches, and $9.75 for everyone else (seniors 60 and older get in for $6.75.) Season passes are available, and the park offers special discounts after 3:00 P.M. and every Sunday evening from mid-July to mid-August; these Sunday Family Nights cost $12 for a family of three people, with each additional family member entering for $3.50. Note that admission includes the use of single inner tubes, body boards, and life vests ($5 refundable deposit required for life vests.) Lockers cost $1.50. Parking is free.

Only one rider at a time is permitted on the Flow Rider Wave, making it quite safe for beginners.

Although this park is smaller than Knott's Soak City, it offers several high-speed slides (42-inch height requirement), a gentle "river" ride, a Children's Water Playground, and a small slide for small fry. Perhaps the star attraction at The Wave is the Flow Rider, a continuous artificial **body-boarding wave**, extremely popular with young surfers-in-training.

No food or drink may be brought into the park; food stands are available throughout the campus.

This water park is owned and operated by the City of Vista, and is extremely family-friendly, offering a number of special family-oriented programs through the season.

Kids love waterparks. Adults do, too!

☆ Sengme Oaks Water Park (North County Inland)

760-742-1921; www.lajollaindians.com. Located on Highway 76, just a few miles past the Palomar Mountain turnoff. From I-15, take the Highway 76 turnoff and go east for 28 miles. The water park will be on your right.

Open Memorial Day to Labor Day, Wednesday through Sunday, 10:00 A.M. to 6:00 P.M.

Admission is free for children age 2 and under, $7.95 for children under 48 inches in height, and $11.95 general admission. Season passes are available, and discount coupons are available in family-oriented publications such as "San Diego Family" and "San Diego Parent." Parking is free; lockers are $3.

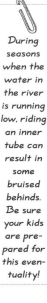

During seasons when the water in the river is running low, riding an inner tube can result in some bruised behinds. Be sure your kids are prepared for this eventuality!

This is the smallest and most casual of San Diego County's three water parks, but it is nestled in a beautiful setting and offers several large high-speed slides (48 inch height requirement) as well as a huge activity pool and a couple of small slides for small fry. There is a snack bar on the premises, but **you are permitted to bring your own food in**, and the park provides **picnic tables** and barbecues. Right next door is the La Jolla Indian River **Campground** ($15 per vehicle per night for camping.) It sits on the San Luis Rey River, nature's own water park! You can rent inner tubes for $5 each and go tubing through the river's gentle current.

Excursions on Land

Trains, Planes, and Trolleys

☆ **The San Diego Trolley** (San Diego, East County, South County)

The cheerful red San Diego Trolley is not really an amusement ride, but an integral part of San Diego's public transportation system. Like San Francisco's cable cars, however, it has also become something of a tourist attraction and makes for a tour that kids love. Many of San Diego's most popular attractions are right on the trolley line, including Qualcomm Stadium, San Diego Mission de Alcalá, Old Town, Seaport Village, and the attractions along Harbor Drive (the Maritime Museum, Seaport Village, and the pier for Harbor tours and the Coronado Ferry.) Fares vary from $1 to $2.25 depending on the distance traveled. On weekends, two children ages 18 and under ride free for each paying adult. Many trolley stations have free parking. For details, call 619-595-4949 or 1-800-COMMUTE; or visit www. sandiego.com and follow the links to the trolley.

☆ **Old Town Trolley Tours** (San Diego and South County)

Unlike the San Diego Trolley, these open-air tour trolleys are tourist-oriented with entertaining and informative tour guides. They cover a two-hour swath of San Diego's finest, including Old Town, the Embarcadero, Seaport Village, Downtown, Coronado, and Balboa Park. For one price, you can get off wherever you wish, spend time sightseeing, playing, shopping, or eating, and then get back on the trolley later. Prices are $8 for children age 4 to 12, $20 for adults. Children under 4 ride free. Call 619-298-8687 for further information.

☆ Amtrak and The Coaster (North County Coastal and San Diego)

The Amtrak and Coaster trains are no more for amusement than is the San Diego Trolley; still, most kids love a train ride!

A particularly scenic ride, and one that's short enough not to tax the attention span of little ones, is the stretch of track between Solana Beach and Oceanside. The train depots at both Oceanside and Solana Beach are within easy walking distance

of the beach; you can combine a train ride along the coast with a beach excursion and avoid the parking hassles. San Diego's downtown Santa Fe Depot is close to Seaport Village and the Embarcadero. It's also a convenient spot to transfer to a trolley for other destinations.

Fares on the Coaster are significantly lower than fares on Amtrak, and children 5 years of age and under travel free with an adult. However, the Coaster does not run on Sundays, and on Saturdays it has a reduced schedule. For information on Amtrak, call 1-800-USA-RAIL; for the Coaster, call 1-800-262-7837. Information on trolleys, buses, and the Coaster can be obtained by calling 1-800-COMMUTE.

☆ San Diego Railroad Museum (East County)

619-595-3030 (weekdays); 619-478-9937 (weekends); www.sdrm.org. 31123½ Highway 94, Campo. The depot is about an hour from downtown San Diego. From I-8 exit Buckman Springs Rd. and go south for about 10 miles. The road ends at Highway 94; turn right and go about 1½ miles. Cross the tracks, turn left at the first street (Forrest Gate Rd.) and left again at the second driveway. Follow the signs to the parking area.

Has your child read *The Little Engine that Could* or is he/she a fan of Thomas the Tank Engine? Treat yourselves to a ride on a real old-time steam engine, or a slightly more modern diesel locomotive. Two trips depart each weekend from Campo to Miller Creek, covering the 32-mile round trip in 90 minutes (two hours for the steam train) and winding through some of San Diego County's most pristine back country. There is a snack bar on board, and kids are permitted to walk through the cars and/or stand at the railing on the caboose to watch the tracks fall away in the distance. Fares are $12 for adults, $3 for children age 6 to 12; add an extra $5 for the steam engine ride. Kids under 6 travel free. Excursions depart at 11:00 A.M. and 2:30 P.M. each Saturday and Sunday from the Campo depot. Reservations are not necessary.

☆ McClellan-Palomar Airport (North County Coastal)

Yarrow Rd., Carlsbad; 760-431-4646. From I-5, take the Palomar Airport Rd. exit and go east 3½ miles, the turn left on Yarrow Rd. Parking is free.
   Hours: By appointment.

The Airport Café is a great spot to grab a light meal or a snack while watching planes take off and land.

Take a **free** tour of the airport conducted by a retired aerospace engineer, and sit in the cockpit of a small plane. Your youngster will get an airplane coloring book and a set of wings.

Other Land Excursions

☆ Stewart Gem Mine (North County Inland)

760-742-1356; www.mmmgems. com. From I-5 or I-15, take Highway 76 east to the village of Pala. Turn left on Magee, and then make the first quick left onto the mine's property.
   Hours: Thursday through Saturday 10:00 A.M. to 4:00 P.M.; Sunday 11:00 A.M. to 3:00 P.M.

Young children will enjoy the chance to get their hands dirty, but may lose interest after an hour or so. Older kids can really get into the excitement of discovery, and can easily make a day of it.

Would you like to be a miner, and discover the shining treasures hidden in the earth's core? At the Stewart Gem Mine on the Pala Indian Reservation in North County, families can experience the excitement of "striking it rich." You can purchase a bucket of dirt from the mine, and they will provide you with screens, water, and trays. Then roll up your sleeves and start sifting—you are guaranteed to go home with some nuggets of tourmaline, the main product of the Stewart Mine. It's a particularly rewarding family experience, since adults and children are equally suited to the task. The little store has a soft drink machine and a shady porch where you can take a break; **bring your own lunch** and stay; you won't want to quit. One bucket of dirt, which is enough for a family to use for a full day, costs $50.

☆ Eagle and High Peak Mines (North County Inland)

End of C Street, off Main Street in Julian. 760-765-0036.
Hours: 10:00 A.M. to 3:00 P.M. daily.
Admission: Children under 5 years of age $1; children 5 years to 15 years $3; adults $7.

Your family can tour one of Julian's original gold mines, dating from 1870; after the tour, you can pan for gold yourself! Although you're not permitted to keep what you find, it's still fun to try your luck as a prospector.

Amusement Centers

☆ Belmont Park

West Mission Bay Drive and Mission Boulevard in Mission Beach; 858-488-1549.
Hours: Sunday through Thursday, 11:00 A.M. to 8:00 P.M.; Friday and Saturday to 10:00 P.M.
Park admission and parking are free; rides are priced separately (see below).

Talk about old timers: This San Diego landmark has been around since 1925! Its most famous attraction is the **Giant Dipper Roller Coaster**.

The park includes other rides and attractions—bumper cars, a tilt-a-whirl, a "submarine" ride, a carousel, a giant trampoline,

The roller coaster has a 50-inch height requirement. Measure your youngster ahead of time, and don't even discuss the Giant Dipper if he/she can't go on it!

and Pirate's Cove, a 3,000 square-foot indoor playground for kids with tunnels and slides filled with bright-colored plastic balls. There's also an arcade game center and a full food court.

Belmont Park's newest attraction is **The Wave**, a simulated ocean wave that surfers of all expertise levels can ride for a fee ($20 per person.) It's gotten excellent reviews from the region's top surfing champions; **note**, however, that it is only open on a seasonal basis.

This family-friendly amusement center is right on the beach; you can combine an af-

Young body surfers or body boarders should watch out for the bigger more aggressive riders of The Wave.

ternoon of sand and surf with an evening of amusements for a special family outing.

Admission to Pirate's Cove is $4.50 for children under 3, $6.50 for children 3 to 12. Two adult chaperones per child are admitted free. The price for the other rides, including the Giant Dipper but excluding The Wave, range from $1.50 to $3.50. During the summer, every Tuesday from 4:00 P.M. till closing, all rides except the trampoline and The Wave are only 75 cents.

☆ Boomers (County-wide)

6999 Clairemont Mesa Blvd. in San Diego; .858-560-4212.
830 Dan Way in Escondido; 760-741-1326.
1525 West Vista Way in Vista; 760-945-9474.
1155 Graves Ave. in El Cajon; 619-593-1155.

All of these family-oriented amusement parks offer miniature golf, bumper boats, batting cages, go-karts, arcade games, and special areas for **tiny tots**. The centers in San Diego and in Vista also offer **Laser Tag**. They open around 11:00 A.M. on weekdays and 9:00 A.M. on weekends; but call individual centers for exact hours. **Admission** is free; you pay for each attraction separately. Prices range from $2 for an individual ride to $5.75 for a round of miniature golf. All-day passes are available at reduced rates.

☆ Chuck E. Cheese (County-wide)

These establishments are more entertainment than restaurant, so we include them here under the category of Amusements. There are shows, games, rides, and lots of noise, as well as pizza. **Admission** is free, and food prices are reasonable.

Look for coupons in the "Pennysaver" (a free local weekly publication).

There are six locations throughout San Diego County, as follows:

9840 Hilbert St., San Diego; 858-578-5860
3146 Sports Arena Blvd., San Diego; 619-523-4385
2481 Vista Way, Oceanside; 760-439-1444
624 W. Mission Ave., Escondido; 760-741-5505
5500 Grossmont Center Drive, La Mesa; 619-698-4351
Highland Ave., National City; 619-474-6667

☆ Fun-4-All Family Entertainment Center (South County)

950 Industrial Blvd., Chula Vista; 619-427-1473.
Hours: Monday through Thursday from 11:00 A.M. to 10:00 P.M.; Saturdays 9:00 A.M. to midnight, Sundays 9:00 A.M. to 10:00 P.M.

Admission is free; attractions are priced separately and range from $1 (20 pitches in the batting cage, a bat and a helmet) to $5 for a round of miniature golf for an adult ($4 for a child under 12.) There are also bumper boat rides and other family-friendly attractions.

☆ The Boardwalk (East County)

1286 Fletcher Parkway, El Cajon; 619-449-7800
Hours: Variable. Call above number for current hours.
Admission is free; rides are each priced separately. Unlimited rides cost $4.45 during the week, $5.45 on weekends. Attractions include a carousel, crazy cars, video games, and a soft play area for little ones.

☆ **Poway Entertainment Center** (North County Inland)

12941 Poway Road, Poway; 858-748-9110 or
www.poway.com.

This is a bowling alley plus, with bumper bowling for little ones, family bowling nights on the weekends, and a Lazer Tag room. Call for hours and prices.

☆ **Arcades**

There are lots of amusement arcades throughout the county where kids can try their skill at video games. We mention three here for their special attractions.

- **Nickel City** at 11610 Carmel Mountain Rd. in the Scripps Ranch area features numerous games for just 5 cents each. Coupons are often available in family publications for free nickels. Call 858-675-9700 for details.

- **Tilt** in Mission Valley Center (1640 Camino del Rio North in San Diego) features old-fashion video games. Call 619-294-3285 for details.

Tours

There are many businesses and local attractions that offer tours for classes and groups; some require advance notice to schedule. The handful of tours listed below are a few of those that are available to individual families as well as to groups, and that represent the most fun for the most kids.

☆ **SeaWorld** (San Diego)

Sea World offers a 90 minute behind-the-scenes tour where you can see how the creatures are trained and cared for when they are not on display. The cost is $5.00 for adults and $4.00 for children. Tours can be arranged by calling 619-222-6363.

☆ The Zoo and the Wild Animal Park (San Diego and North County Inland)

The Zoo and Wild Animal Park offer a variety of different tours ranging from "behind-the-scenes" peeks into animals' bedrooms to specialized tours of specific attractions. Most of these tours come in two versions, one designed for families with children from 4 years to 9 years of age, and one for 10-year-olds through adults. For more information and reservations call 619-557-3963. Prices vary with the tour, but are always lower for members of the Zoologic Society.

☆ ARCO U.S. Olympic Training Center (South County)

Free tours are offered daily, departing every hour on the hour in the morning, and every hour on the half-hour in the afternoon. This attraction is discussed in more detail in Chapter 9.

☆ Helen Woodward Animal Center (North County Coastal)

If you have an animal lover in the family, check out the once-a-month tour offered free at this very special animal care center. See Chapter 8 for the classes offered here for kids. The Center is located in Rancho Santa Fe at 6461 El Apajo Road. For details, call 858-756-4117 or visit their website at www.animalcenter.org.

☆ Waste Management (East County)

There was a time when touring a waste management plant might have sounded less than glamorous. In these times of environmental consciousness, however, waste management may be one of the planet's most important jobs! Besides, some kids find the **giant trash trucks** and their muscular drivers to be a source of fascination. You can have a free tour of the facilities at 1001 West Bradley in El Cajon by making an appointment in advance. Call 619-596-5100.

Adventures through the Year—Calendar of Events

Those who come to San Diego from other parts of the country often believe that southern California has no seasons. But those who live here come to appreciate the rhythm of the southern California year. It is true that we are blessed with a mild climate all year; most of the adventures described in this book can be enjoyed at any time. But it is also true that each season has its own special flavor and offers its own unique adventures to children and their families.

Below is a listing by month of some of those annual events most attractive to children. There are two publications that come out monthly and that publish day-by-day calendars of things to do with kids; they are **wonderful resources** for San Diego families or for visitors. One is the *San Diego Family Magazine* (their website is at www. sandiegofamily .com, 619-685- 6970) and the other is the *San Diego Parent* (619-624-2770, website at www. parenthoodweb. com). Both are available free at your local library and at many other locations that serve children and families—at McDonald's, Blockbuster Video stores, Longs Drug Stores, Play Co. toy stores, Dairy Queen, and more. *The San Diego Reader*, a weekly free publication also available at libraries and many other locations, has an entire Calendar section with a special weekly subheading entitled "For Kids." It's **another terrific resource**. You can find them on the web, too, at www. sandiegoreader.com.

Note: Throughout the year, many communities sponsor their own local street fairs, carnivals, and festivals. We have not

included those in this list, but we encourage families to check
their own local newspapers, or the resources mentioned
above, for upcoming neighborhood events.

January

❀ Whale watching season gets under way. See Chapter 3,
"Beach and Bay Adventures," for details. Cabrillo National
Monument hosts an entire Whale Watching Weekend for
families. Call them at 619-557-5450. *(South County, San
Diego, and North County Coastal.)*

❀ Martin Luther King Jr. Day Parade downtown. Parents
and kids are invited to march in the parade. For details,
call 619-264-0542. *(San Diego)*

❀ Teddy Bear, Doll, and Toy Festival. If you or your children
have a serious interest in teddy bears or antique dolls, this
is a great opportunity to join professional collectors in
viewing the best of the market. The exposition takes place
at the Scottish Rite Temple, 1895 Camino del Rio South.
Call 760-434-7444 for details. There is an **admission** fee
of $5.00. *(San Diego)*

❀ Young Eagle Flight Day at Brown Field. Kids between the
ages of 7 and 15 learn the basics of flight safety, then
have a chance to fly. Brown Field is at 1500 Heritage
Road in Otay Mesa. The event is free. Call 619-421-6546
for details. *(South County)*

February

❀ San Diego Padres Spring Training Camp opens in Peoria,
Arizona. This is a great opportunity to see some
professional baseball for a fraction of the cost of tickets
during the regular season. Even better, you can really get
"up close and personal" with the players during these very
informal games. Peoria is just a short drive from the
airport in Phoenix; or you can drive there from San Diego

in about 6 hours. Call for game schedules and tickets at 619-29PADRES, or visit their website at www.padres.com.

❀ Wild flowers begin to bloom in Anza-Borrego State Park. Call the wildflower hotline at 760-767-4684 for updated information on the best week to catch Mother Nature's show. *(90 miles east of San Diego)*

❀ Chinese New Year celebration at Third Avenue and J St. You can enjoy displays of martial arts, traditional Chinese dancers, crafts booths, and—of course—great food. Call 619-234-7844 for exact dates (**note** that the Chinese calendar is a lunar one; sometimes Chinese New Year falls in January!). *(San Diego)*

❀ Vietnamese Tet Festival at 2160 Ulric Street in San Diego. You'll appreciate the beautiful ethnic clothing and food, the games, martial arts, and dance. Call 619-277-6147 for more information. *(San Diego)*

❀ Youth Fishing Derby at Lake Poway (858-679-5465). See Chapter 4 for more details on Lake Poway. *(North County Inland)*

March

❀ Ocean Beach Kite Festival, Ocean Beach Recreation Center. Make your own kite, or bring a store-bought kite, or just come to watch! Festival includes a parade of participants to the beach. Call 619-224-0189 for more information. *(San Diego)*

❀ St. Patrick's Day Parade at Sixth Avenue in San Diego. If you love the "Riverdance" style Celtic dances, you'll enjoy this Irish celebration. The parade is followed by an Irish festival in Balboa Park. Call 619-268-9111 or 619-299-7812 for details. *(San Diego)*

❀ Pegleg Liar's Contest, Anza-Borrego State Park. This annual yarn-spinning contest is held in honor of Pegleg Smith, a legendary gold miner from the last century.

Anyone can enter; or you can simply gather around the campfire and listen to the tall tales. Call 760-767-5311 for details. *(90 miles east of San Diego)*

❀ Junior Carlsbad Run. This event is for kids only, from age 12 on down to the diaper set. There is an entry fee. Call 858-450-6510 or visit the website at www.eliteracing.com for details. *(North County Coastal)*

❀ Arbor Day at the Wild Animal Park. Kids under 11 years old get into the Wild Animal Park free when accompanied by an adult. In exchange for the free admission, you will be invited to plant a tree—an honor in this beautiful setting. Call 760-738-4100 for more information. *(North County Inland)*

❀ March 31 is the birthday of César Chávez, one of California's great native sons. A parade and fiesta is held in his honor in San Diego, complete with rousing live music and wonderful food. Call 619-238-0314 for details of time and place. *(San Diego)*

❀ There is a big auto show at the San Diego Convention Center. Great for families with car enthusiasts! Call 619-525-5959. *(San Diego)*

❀ March is the month when local family-oriented publications begin reviewing summer programs for kids (camps, classes, etc.) Check the *San Diego Family Magazine* or *San Diego Parent* magazine this month, and for the next couple of months, for a wealth of information on summertime adventures. See the introductory paragraphs to this appendix for details on these publications. *(Available county-wide)*

April

❀ Celebrate Earth Day at Balboa Park's EarthFair. There are activities for kids all day, including face painting, storytelling, and a Children's Stage. Free shuttles depart frequently from Florida Canyon; don't even think about trying to park in the Park! Call 858-496-6666 for details. *(San Diego)*

❀ Kids' Day at the Carlsbad Flower Fields. Moms and dads can enjoy the splendor of the colorful Carlsbad flower fields while the children are entertained by clowns, rides, food, balloons, and fun. There is an admission charge. Call 760-930-9123 for details. *(North County Coastal)*

❀ Children's Day in the Park is an annual event sponsored by the San Diego Association for the Education of Young Children. Balboa Park buzzes with arts and crafts, magic shows, storytelling, and lots of resource information for parents. Call 858-565-1653. *(San Diego)*

❀ Lakeside Western Days and Rodeo at Highway 67 and Maple View in Lakeside. In addition to a real western-style rodeo, you'll be treated to parades and school band concerts. **General admission** is $8, reserved seating is $11, and kids under 12 get in free. Call 858-292-0092 or 619-561-4331. *(East County)*

❀ Most communities sponsor **Easter egg hunts** for local children. Call your own Department of Parks and Recreation, or consult one of the calendar resources listed in the introduction to this appendix. Additionally, San Diego's Gaslamp Quarter hosts an annual **Easter Hat Parade**, which always includes an appearance by the Easter Bunny. Call 619-233-5227 for more information.

May

❀ Cinco de Mayo festivals take place all over the county, celebrating our Mexican heritage. They include Old Town (619-296-3161 or 619-220-5422), the Embarcadero on Harbor Drive in San Diego (619-235-4013), Grape Day Park in Escondido (760-432-2893), the Oceanside Pier Amphitheater in Oceanside (760-839-6568), and downtown Chula Vista (619-422-1982). *(Old Town and the Embarcadero are in the San Diego region; Escondido is*

North County Inland; Oceanside is North County Coastal; and Chula Vista is South County.)

❀ National City Maytime Band Review Parade. Junior High and High School bands from all over southern California contribute the rousing music to this high-stepping parade. A cheerleading competition follows. Grandstand seating costs $2. Call 619-477-9339. *(South County)*

❀ Dr. Seuss Kids' Magic Mile Run/Walk. Like the Carlsbad Jr. Run, this is a running event designed especially for children. The course is in the former Naval Training Center in Point Loma; there is an entry fee. Call 858-792-2900 or check out the website at www.ut-drseuss8k.com. *(San Diego)*

❀ Buds 'n' Blooms Kids Day at Balboa Park offers scavenger hunts, a funky hat parade, and crafts—all centered around a flower theme. Call 619-239-0512. *(San Diego)*

❀ Cupa Days Celebration at the Pala Indian Reservation is a weekend-long festival of songs, dances, games, crafts, and food. The Pala Reservation is east of I-15 off of Highway 76; it's beautiful rural San Diego County at its finest. Call 760-742-1590. *(North County Inland)*

❀ Ramona Round-Up Rodeo in the Fred Grand Arena in Ramona. This is another rip-roaring Western-style rodeo, complete with bronco riders, bull riders, steer ropers, and plenty of fun. Call 760-789-1484. *(North County Inland)*

❀ Founders' Day at the Wild Animal Park. The second Wednesday in May is Founders' Day at the Wild Animal Park; this means that **admission** is **free** for everyone! All you have to do is show up. *(North County Inland)*

June

❀ Southern California Exposition (better known locally as the Del Mar Fair.) Lasting till July 4, this three-week-long fair includes exhibits of animals and plants, a midway with games and amusement rides, lots of food and entertainment, and special events daily. Call 858-755-1161 or 858-793- 5555, or visit www.delmarfair. com. Be sure to take sunscreen, plenty of water, and comfortable shoes. *(North County Coastal)*

❀ Corpus Christi Fiesta at the Pala Mission. Call 760-742-3317. Treat your family to a beautiful back country drive and the peaceful atmosphere of the Pala Mission. The fiesta includes carnivals, kids' games, wonderful food, and a stirring procession. Children can bring their pets for the Blessing of the Animals. *(North County Inland)*

❀ Indian Fair, Museum of Man, Balboa Park. 619-239-2001. A Native American "exposition," this fair offers lots of hands-on experiences for children including music, games, dancing, and Native American food. **Admission** is $6 for adults, $3 for kids from ages 6 to 17. Kids under 6 get in free. *(San Diego)*

❀ Threshing Bee and Antique Engine Show. 760-941-1791. The Antique Gas and Steam Engine Museum in Vista comes to life as the engines are cranked up and local experts exhibit old-time skills such as log-sawing and black-smithing. There is music, folk dancing, and a shady park for picnicking. There is an admission price. See Chapter 7 for more details. *(North County Coastal)*

❀ Greek Festival at the Sprydion Greek Orthodox Church, 3655 Park Boulevard in San Diego. Greek music gets everyone dancing! Add to that the irresistible fragrance of Greek food and the family-friendly atmosphere, and you have yourself a terrific outing. Call 619-297-4165. *(San Diego)*

The fair is not an inexpensive event. There is a parking fee, an admission fee, and a fee for the amusement rides. Check for current prices before setting out! Albertson's super market often has discount coupons for the Fair; also, call the number above to inquire about Wristband Days, when kids can ride on all the rides for the price of one wristband.

❀ Scottish Highland Games in Brengle Terrace Park in Vista. Bagpipe music in San Diego County? You bet! Not only that, but you'll see some wonderful Highland Flings, eat some great Scottish delicacies, and watch the amazing athletic competitions that are traditional to these games. Call 619-645-8080 for details or visit www.sdhighlandgames.org. *(North County Inland)*

❀ Portuguese Festa at 2818 Addison Street in San Diego. One of the oldest ethnic celebrations in town, this lively event includes music, fabulous Portuguese dancing, a parade, and lots of mouth-watering food. Call 619-223-5880. *(San Diego)*

❀ Clown Day in Julian. If you have a youngster who's into clowns, don't miss this annual event at Main St. and 3rd Ave. in Julian. Clowns roam the streets offering magic tricks, balloons, face-painting, and more. The event ends by 2:30, so plan to get there early. *(North County Inland)*

❀ Grunion Festival. The famous grunion fish are the focus of this early-summer event in Pacific Beach just south of Crystal Pier. Native American singers and dancers as well as local lore and food make for a good time, even if the grunion don't show up! Call 858-274-1326. *(San Diego)*

❀ Check out the Soap Box Derby in San Diego. Call 619-239-4175. *(San Diego)*

❀ **School's out**, and many of San Diego's year-round attractions add special summer-time features starting in June. **Belmont Park** in Mission Beach (858-488-1549) offers Family Nights every Tuesday, with many rides (including the Giant Dipper) for only seventy-five cents. **The Zoo** begins its Nighttime Zoo Program (619-234-3153) and the **Wild Animal Park** offers The Park at Dark (760-480-0100). All of the public **libraries** have summer reading programs for kids; check with your local branch library for details. The **County Parks Department** sponsors periodic evening storytelling events at various county parks; call 858-694-3049. In addition, many family-friendly, free activities begin to bloom around town as the days get longer and lazier. A partial list follows.

- Free Outdoor Cinema

  The Star of India (part of the Maritime Museum in San Diego—see Chapter 7) offers evening **"Movies Before the Mast,"** family-oriented films shown in a beautiful outdoor setting. Call 619-234-9153. Cox Communications hosts its **Sunset Cinema** series of free movies at outdoor venues around the county. Call 619-263-9251 or visit them at www.cox.com/sandiego. The Garden Cabaret offers **Cinema Under the Stars** at University Town Center *(San Diego)* near the skating rink. Call 619-295-4221. The San Diego Public Library in downtown San Diego presents **Saturday Movie Madness** with full-length feature films for children (1:00 P.M.) and teens (3:00 P.M.) every Saturday afternoon. Call 619-236-5838.

- Free Outdoor Music

  Many of San Diego's communities offer free concerts in local parks during the summer. Call your own community services department for details on your local free music scene. Below is just a brief sampling; it is by no means inclusive!

  Balboa Park's Spreckels Organ Pavilion, Tuesdays, Wednesdays, and Thursdays 6:15 to 7:15 A variety of free concerts is offered here during the summer, in addition to the year-round program of organ concerts on Sundays at 2:00 P.M. Call 619-239-0512. *(San Diego)*

  Carlsbad's TGIF Jazz in the Park Fridays from 6:00 to 8:00 P.M. at various parks. Call 760-434-2904. *(North County Coastal)*

  La Jolla Concerts by the Sea Sundays from 2:00 P.M. to 4:00 P.M. at Scripps Park (Coast Boulevard and Girard Ave.) Call 619-645-8115. *(San Diego)*

  El Cajon's Concerts on the Green every Friday at the Prescott Promenade on Main Street from 5:30 to 7:30 P.M. Some evenings offer special activities for children. Call 619-401-8858. *(East County)*

Chula Vista Concerts in the Park on Sundays at 4:00 in Memorial Park at 385 Park Way. Call 619-691-5071. *(South County)*

❀ Summer Camp Planning: Be sure to check out the wonderful camp programs offered by some of San Diego's non-profit institutions, in addition to the for-profit camps that abound. The Zoo, the Wild Animal Park, and many of the museums in Balboa Park have great summer adventures. The Zoo and the Wild Animal Park have special programs for **teens**, as does the San Diego Museum of Natural History. All of the YMCAs have summer programs for all interest levels. The San Diego Humane Society *(San Diego)* and the Helen Woodward Animal Care Center *(North County Coastal)* have special programs for kids interested in animals.

July

❀ Independence Day Celebrations. From San Ysidro to Oceanside, many communities sponsor events for the Fourth of July, including fireworks displays. Check your local newspaper for your closest "sky show." Common sites for fireworks include the following list. Always call ahead, as the list may vary from year to year.

- **East County**—Viejas Casino in Alpine, John F. Kennedy Park in El Cajon, Lake Murray in La Mesa, Spring Valley Swap Meet in Spring Valley.

- **North County Inland**—Poway High School in Poway, Ramona High School in Ramona, Rancho Bernardo High School in Rancho Bernardo, Bradley Park in San Marcos, Valley Center High School in Valley Center, Brengle Terrace Park in Vista.

- **North County Coastal**—LEGOLAND in Carlsbad, Del Mar Fairgrounds in Del Mar, south side of Oceanside Pier in Oceanside.

- **San Diego**—La Jolla Shores in La Jolla, Memorial Park in Logan Heights, Mira Mesa Community Park in Mira Mesa, SeaWorld in Mission Bay, Qualcomm Stadium in Mission Valley, Ocean Beach Pier in Ocean Beach.

- **South County**—J Street Marina in Chula Vista, Glorietta Bay in Coronado, Kimball Park in National City, Larson Field in San Ysidro.

❀ Festival of the Bells, Mission San Diego de Alcalá. The annual birthday celebration for this old San Diego landmark features rides, games, shows, and the Blessing of the Animals, to which children may bring their pets. Call 619-283-7319 for details. *(San Diego)*

❀ Sand Castle Competition, Imperial Beach. What was once an informal local tradition has become a major event, with sand castle contestants coming from far and wide and creating some incredible works of art at the foot of the Imperial Beach Pier. There is a separate contest just for kids, and there is a parade and fireworks, too. You don't have to enter the contest to come and enjoy the fun. Call 619-424-6663 for details. *(South County)*

❀ Pacific Islander Festival at the former Naval Training Center. Call 619-699-8797 or visit www.pacificislanders.com for details. The cultures, food, crafts, and customs of Melanesia, Micronesia, and Polynesia are featured at this weekend-long event. **Admission** is free. *(San Diego)*

❀ Obon Festival. Japanese culture is the centerpiece of this celebration at the Vista Buddhist Temple and Community Center. **Admission** is free. Call 760-941-8800. *(North County Coastal)*

❀ Summer Organ Festival begins in Balboa Park, with free organ concerts every Monday evening at the open-air Spreckels Organ Pavilion at 7:30. Call 619-239-0512. *(San Diego)*

❀ Del Mar Horseracing season begins, lasting through Labor Day. Although horse racing is generally not really a family activity, each Saturday and Sunday is a **Family Fun Day** at the track. The infield offers pony rides, face painting, inflatable jumps, a giant slide, and more. **Admission** and activities are all free for children under 17, accompanied by parent or guardian. Call 858-793-5533 or visit www.delmarracing.com. *(North County Coastal)*

Bring lawn or beach chairs, a picnic lunch, and even an umbrella if you want to, and set up in the infield to watch the horses.

❀ Civil War re-enactment at the Rancho Guajome Adobe in Vista. Call 858-694-3049 for details.

August

❀ Barona Indian Reservation Barbecue. Dancing, singing, crafts, and plenty of fresh, delicious food are some of the highlights of this event at the Barona Mission. Like the other Mission Festivals, this one also includes a special Blessing of the Animals. Call 619-744-4318. *(East County)*

❀ Latin American Festival at the Bazaar del Mundo in Old Town. On the first weekend in August, you'll find music, dancing, food, and crafts from all over the Americas creating a banquet for the senses. Call 619-296-3266 for details. *(San Diego)*

❀ The Philippine Cultural Arts Festival takes place in Balboa Park. It's free, and you'll be treated to music, dance, crafts, kids' games, and lots of wonderful food. Call 619-444-7528. *(San Diego)*

❀ Fleet Week is a time when the public is invited to tour the U.S. Navy ships that call San Diego home. Call 619-544-1338. *(San Diego)*

September

❀ Día de la Independencia (Mexican Independence Day) celebrations. There is a big fiesta in Old Town (619-291-4903) and another in Kimball Park in National City, sponsored by Radio Latina (619-575-9090.) Don't miss the chance to get in on these colorful celebrations of Mexico's independence from Spain. *(Old Town is in the San Diego region, and National City is in the South County region.)*

❀ California American Indian Day Celebration, Balboa Park. Native Americans representing different tribes from all over California gather at the Museum of Man to exhibit their crafts, food, music, and dance. There are plenty of interactive experiences for children and their families. **Admission** is free. Call 619-281-5964. *(San Diego)*

❀ Cabrillo Festival, Cabrillo National Monument, Point Loma. In honor of the first European to discover California, a re-enactment of Juan Cabrillo's landing is presented along with music, food, and entertainment. Call 619-281-5964 for more information. *(San Diego)*

❀ Greek Festival at St. Constantine and Helen Greek Orthodox Church in Cardiff-by-the-Sea. Call 760-942-0920 to enjoy this feast for the senses. There is a $2 **admission** charge for adults; kids under the age of 12 get in free. *(North County Coastal)*

❀ Julian Apple Harvest. It's always fun to take the family to Julian, but September is when the apples are fresh from the trees, the smell of apple pie is in the air, and jugs of fresh apple cider are everywhere. There are a few farms in Julian that will still allow families to pick their own apples. Call 760-765-1857. *(North County Inland)*

❀ Poway Rodeo. Lakeside and Ramona have their rodeos, and so does Poway—and a great one it is! Call 858-736-0594. *(North County Inland)*

❀ Bayfair on Mission Bay with boat races, and extreme
sports show, games, and fireworks. **Admission** is from
$15 to $30. Call 619-225-9160. *(San Diego)*

❀ Harbor Days are celebrated in Chula Vista at the Chula
Vista Yacht Harbor (619-426-2882) and in Oceanside at
the Oceanside Pier (760-722-1534.) Both events are free
and include music, food, and—in Oceanside—a fishing
derby. *(Chula Vista is in the South County region, and
Oceanside is in the North County Coastal region.)*

October

❀ October is Children's Month at the San Diego Zoo. Kids
under 12 years old are admitted **free** all month. On
Founders' Day, the first Monday in October, **admission** is
free for everyone. Call 619-234-3153. *(San Diego)*

❀ Air Show at the Miramar Marine Corps Air Station. Military
pilots put on a fabulous display of precision and stunt
flying for the public. The highlight is the appearance of
the famous Blue Angels who evoke gasps of admiration
from their earth-bound audience. Call 858-577-1000 for
details. Parking and **admission** are free, but get there
early, bring lawn chairs, umbrellas for the sun, sunscreen,
and water. There is a **twilight show** on Saturday evening
for those who prefer to wait out the heat of the day. *(San
Diego)*

❀ Threshing Bee and Antique Engine Show (See June).
(North County Coastal)

❀ Cal State San Marcos Pow Wow. This free Native
American event includes inter-tribal dancing, drum
demonstrations, native food, and crafts. Call
760-750-4011 for details. *(North County Inland)*

❀ Oktoberfest in El Cajon. This annual event is put on by
the German American Societies of San Diego, and
includes live entertainment, food, and games. **Admission**

is free for anyone under 21 years of age; others pay $1 admission. Call 619-442-6637. *(East County)*

❀ Virtually all communities have lots of child-oriented activities for **Halloween**. Check your local elementary school for Halloween carnivals and your local Department of Parks and Recreation for other seasonal events. Some of the big Halloween events in the county include, but are not limited to, the following:

- The "Haunted Museum" at the Museum of Man in Balboa Park. There is an admission fee. Call 619-239-2001 for details. *(San Diego)*

- The "Trail of Terror" in Balboa Park at Marston Point, east of 6th and Juniper. There is an admission fee. Call 619-231-0261. *(San Diego)*

- The Haunted Aquarium at the Stephen Birch Aquarium in La Jolla. Advanced reservations required for all activities. Call 858-534-3474. *(San Diego)*

- Children's Museum/Museo de los Niños in downtown San Diego offers a Halloween Hoopla and Día de los Muertos celebration. **Admission** is $6 for anyone over 2 years old. Call 619-233-KIDS. *(San Diego)*

- LEGOLAND's Brick-or-Treat Celebration. **Admission** is $34 for adults, $29 for kids between the ages of 3 and 16. *(North County Coastal)*

- Frightmare on Market Street (corner of Sixth and Market in downtown San Diego). There is an admission fee. Call 619-231-3611 or visit www.frightmareonmarketst.com. *(San Diego)*

- The Haunted Hotel at the corner of Fourth and Market in downtown San Diego. There is an admission fee. Call 619-231-0131 or visit www.hauntedhotel.com. *(San Diego)*

- The Haunted Star of India at the Maritime Museum on the Embarcadero. Call 619-234-9153. *(San Diego)*

Haunted houses can be truly terrifying to young children. Know your child before you subject him/her to an experience that turns out not to be fun!

181

- Halloween Carnival and Haunted House in Spreckels Park on Coronado. There is a $1.00 fee for admission to the Haunted House; the Carnival is **free**. Call 619-522-7342. *(South County)*

- The **free** Halloween celebration put on by the Self Realization Fellowship in Encinitas (760-753-1811). This party is completely non-denominational and unrelated to religion; it is the temple's annual "thank-you" to the community. Get there early, as it's very popular. *(North County Coastal)*

- Bates Nut Farm and Bell Gardens, both in Valley Center, have big pumpkin farms where you can go to pick out your fresh Halloween pumpkin. Bell Gardens also offers a hay ride, a haunted walk known as Ghost Canyon, and a corn maze. See Chapter 5 for details on both Bates Nut Farm and Bell Gardens. *(Both are in North County Inland.)*

November

❀ Día de los Muertos observance in El Campo Santo (the old cemetery) in Old Town. There are guides to explain this beautiful tradition and to lead you through the festive activities that honor the dead while celebrating life. **Admission** is free. Call 619-491-0110 for details. *(San Diego)*

❀ Mother Goose Parade, West Main Street, El Cajon. Bands, clowns, and floats featuring Mother Goose characters make this parade a fairy tale come true for young children. Call 619-444-8712. *(East County)*

❀ Santee Parade, Town Center Parkway, Santee. Call 619-449-6572. This is one of the traditional "kick-offs" to the holiday season. *(East County)*

❀ Starlight Yule Parade, downtown Chula Vista. Call 619-420-6602. South County families welcome Santa to town at this annual holiday event. *(South County)*

❀ Festival of Lights, Del Mar Fairgrounds. Call
858-793-5555 for admission prices and dates of this
winter fantasyland by the sea. *(North County Coastal)*

❀ Festival of Lights, Old Town. Call 619-296-3161 to enjoy
this holiday festival that features dances from all over the
world. **Admission** is free. *(San Diego)*

December

❀ Christmas on the Prado, Balboa Park. This traditional San
Diego holiday event usually occurs on December 1 and
December 2, and ushers in the Christmas season for
many families. There are carolers, a candlelight
procession, and lots of entertainment. It's a wonderful
evening for parents and kids to share. **Admission** is free.
For details, call 619-239-0512 or 619-235-1100. A word
of warning: Traffic becomes very congested and parking
hard to come by as families flock to this annual event.
Come early, or car pool, or take the bus! *(San Diego)*

❀ Old Town's Las Posadas. One of Mexico's most beautiful
Christmas traditions lives on in this re-enactment of
Joseph and Mary's search for shelter on the first
Christmas Eve. Christmas carols and a "Las Posadas"
procession are followed by a children's piñata party.
Admission is free. Call 619-297-1183 or 619-220-5422.
(San Diego)

❀ Wild Animal Park Festival of Lights. A beautiful holiday
celebration at the Wild Animal Park, this special evening
features Christmas cookie decorating for children, puppet
shows, Christmas caroling and a nighttime "safari." Call
234-6541. *(North County Inland)*

❀ Quail Botanical Gardens in Encinitas offers a holiday
celebration featuring horse-drawn wagon rides,
marshmallow roasting, and professional story telling.
There is a cost for admission, and an additional cost for

the wagon rides. Call 760-436-3036. *(North County Coastal)*

❀ Rancho Christmas at the Rancho Guajome Adobe in Vista. Call 858-694-3049. *(North County Coastal)*

❀ Many of Balboa Park's museums have special holiday events. Watch newspapers or call individual museums for details. (See Chapter 2 for museum phone numbers.) *(San Diego)*

❀ Many communities have Christmas parades and other Christmas events; check your local newspapers. Particularly beautiful are the Parades of Lights that take place on harbors from Oceanside to Chula Vista, as well as on Mission Bay. (Oceanside: 760-966-4570; Mission Bay: 858-488 0501; San Diego and Chula Vista: 619-686-6570.) There is no admission fee to watch the boats turn the water into a winter wonderland. *(Oceanside is in North County Coastal, Mission Bay and San Diego Harbors are both in the San Diego region, and Chula Vista is in the South County.)*

❀ On New Year's Eve, some communities sponsor "First Night" alcohol-free family-oriented events. Two such communities are Escondido *(North County Inland)* and San Diego. For details, including admission cost, call 760-739-0101 for Escondido or 619-296-8731 for San Diego.

During the December holiday season, many neighborhoods have great local light displays on private residences. Check out www.sandiegoinsider.com to find out what's hot in your neighborhood.

Free Adventures

See individual chapters for details of each admission-free adventure.

Chapter 1: The Big Ones

• The San Diego Zoo *(San Diego)*: Children under 12 are admitted free throughout the month of October; everyone is admitted free on Founders' Day, the first Monday in October.

• The Wild Animal Park *(North County Inland)*: Children under 12 are admitted free throughout the month of October; everyone is admitted free on Founders' Day, the second Wednesday in May.

Chapter 2: Balboa Park

• Many attractions in Balboa Park are free *(San Diego)*: the two playgrounds, Spanish Village, House of Pacific Relations, Centro Cultural de la Raza, the Spreckels Organ concerts, picnics on the lawns or by the lily pond, and the street entertainers.

• Balboa Park's museums are free on the following Tuesdays *(San Diego)*:

First Tuesday of the month: The Ruben H. Fleet Science Center, the San Diego Natural History Museum, the Model Railroad Museum

Second Tuesday of the month: The Hall of Champions

Third Tuesday of the month: The Museum of Man, the San Diego Museum of Art

Fourth Tuesday of the month: The Aerospace Musuem, the Automotive Museum

Chapter 3: Beach and Bay Adventures

• All beaches adventures, bay adventures, and tide pool adventures are free, with the exceptions of Torrey Pines State Park beach and the tide pools at the Cabrillo National Monument, both of which require a parking fee *(San Diego)*. Some other beaches have metered parking, but you can often find free street parking nearby.

• All pier-fishing adventures are free, with the exception of Crystal Pier *(San Diego)*, which requires the purchase of a fishing license.

• Looking for grunion is free, but **note** that anyone over the age of 16 years must have a fishing license to collect them. *(South County, San Diego, and North County Coastal)*

• Swimming with leopard sharks at La Jolla Shores is free. *(San Diego)*

Chapter 4: Adventures in Parks and Lakes

• All the local neighborhood parks are free. For help finding your local parks, check the front section of Pacific Bell's Yellow Pages directory under the section called "Regional Parks," or the back section of *The Thomas Guide: San Diego County (County-wide)*

• Mission Trails Regional Park in San Diego *(East County)* and Ellen Scripps

Browning Park in La Jolla *(San Diego)* have no day-use fee. The other parks listed in Chapter 4 have day use fees (usually $2).

• Fishing at Chollas Lake *(San Diego)* is free and is limited to children under the age of 16 years. Fishing at all other lakes listed in Chapter 4 requires a California fishing license and also a day-use permit.

Chapter 5: Adventures in Nature

• All of the trails described in Chapter 5 can be explored free, with the following exceptions: Quail Gardens in Encinitas *(North County Coastal)* has an entrance fee, but is **free** on the first Tuesday of every month; Torrey Pines State Park *(San Diego)*, Cabrillo National Monument *(San Diego)*, and Cuyamaca State Park *(East County)* all have day-use fees (the fees range from $2 to $4 per vehicle.)

• All of North County's lagoons are free.

• All of the "Creatures-to-Meet-and-Greet" adventures described in Chapter 5 are free, with the following exceptions, each of which has an entrance fee: The Monarch Butterfly Program in Encinitas *(North County Coastal)*, the Free Flight Aviary in Del Mar *(North County Coastal)*, the Stephen Birch Aquarium and Museum in La Jolla *(San Diego)*, the Chula Vista Nature Center in Chula Vista *(South County)*, and the Stein Family Farm in National City *(South County)*. Bell Gardens, in Valley Center, is free on weekends only. *(North County Inland)*

Chapter 6: Adventures in Town

• All of the shopping malls listed in Chapter 6 are free; however, Horton Plaza and Seaport Village *(San Diego)* charge a parking fee. You can get the parking fee waived by making a minor purchase and having your parking ticket validated.

• Participation in the Kids' Clubs at participating malls is free. *(County-wide)*

• The Dr. Martin Luther King Jr. Promenade *(San Diego)* is free.

• All the special events at certain children's stores are free (Zany Brainy in *San Diego and East County*, Lakeshore Learning Store in *San Diego*, The Learning Express *in North County Inland* and *North County Coastal.)*

• The specialty store adventures are free (Basic Brown Bear Factory in *San Diego* and Knorr Candle Factory in *North County Coastal.)* **Note**, however, that purchases in these stores are *not* free; for example, you can look around the Basic Brown Bear Factory for nothing, but participating in the creation of your own teddy bear will cost you!

• The Farmers' Markets and Flea Markets listed in Chapter 6 are free. The Swap Meets all charge a minimal entrance fee. *(County-wide)*

• Strolling across the suspension bridges *(San Diego)* is free.

• Participation in Nordstrom's fashion-shows-for-children is free. *(North County Inland, San Diego)*

• Cruisin' Grand Avenue in Escondido on Friday evenings is free. *(North County Inland)*

Chapter 7: Adventures in Time

• Old Town State Historic Park. *(San Diego)*
• The Firehouse Museum. *(San Diego)*
• The Motor Transport Museum. *(East County)*
• The Barona Museum and Cultural Center. *(East County)*
• The "Spirit of Nightfire" show on the Viejas reservation. *(East County)*
• San Pasqual State Historic Park. *(North County Inland)*
• A trip to the historic town of Julian. *(North County Inland)*
• The California Surf Museum. *(North County Coastal)*
• The Dinosaur Gallery. *(North County Coastal)*
• The Hotel del Coronado. *(South County)*

• Ancient rock painting and rock carving in Anza-Borrego State Park. *(90 miles east of San Diego)*
• All of the local historical sites listed at the end of Chapter 7 are free. *(County-wide)*

Chapter 8: Adventures of the Mind

• All activities at public libraries are free. These include story hours for children of all ages, music programs, movies, crafts, free use of computers, and much more. Find your local public library in the Pacific Bell White Pages telephone directory in the "Government" (blue-bordered) section in front, either under the name of your city, or under "County" if you live in an unincorporated part of San Diego County. *(County-wide)*
• Story times, music, crafts, etc. at certain toy stores and book stores are free. These occur county-wide, and are listed in some detail in Chapter 8. *(All regions)*
• The pipe organ concerts in Balboa Park. *(San Diego)*
• The San Diego Youth Master Chorale. *(San Diego)*
• The San Diego Art Institute in Balboa Park is free for children under 12 years of age. Adults get in free on the third Tuesday of each month. *(San Diego)*
• The Museum of Contemporary Art, in La Jolla and in San Diego, is free on the first Sunday and the third Tuesday of each month. *(San Diego)*
• Children's crafts classes at selected Home Depot stores are free. *(All regions)*
• Palomar Observatory on Palomar Mountain *(North County Inland)* is free.
• The Mount Laguna Telescope, on Mount Laguna east of San Diego, is available to the public free of charge on Friday and Saturday evenings during the summer.
• On the first Wednesday of each month, at twilight, the San Diego Astronomy Association sets up telescopes on the plaza in Balboa Park just behind the Ruben H.

Fleet Science Center. There is no charge to look through their telescopes and benefit from their guidance. *(San Diego)*
• Star Parties sponsored by the San Diego Astronomy Association at their site about 75 miles *east of San Diego* are free. See Chapter 8 for details.

Chapter 9: Adventures of the Body

• Free roller skating is available in San Marcos, through their Department of Recreation, on selected Friday evenings in spring and summer. *(North County Inland)*
• There are several free skateboard parks in the county. They include the Washington Street Skate Park *(San Diego)* and the Carlsbad Safety Center *(North County Coastal)*.
• If your family already owns bicycles, a family bicycle outing is, of course, free! You can get a free map of San Diego bicycle routes by calling 619-231-BIKE.
• Visiting the San Diego Chargers' football training camp on the campus of UCSD is free. See Chapter 9 for details. *(San Diego)*

Chapter 10: Excursions, Amusements, Tours

• The tour of the McClellan-Palomar Airport in Carlsbad *(North County Coastal)* is free.
• The tour of the Helen Woodward Animal Center in Rancho Santa Fe *(North County Coastal)* is free.
• The tour of the Waste Management plant in El Cajon *(East County)* is free.

Appendix 1: Adventures through the Year—Calendar of Annual Events

• January—Dr. Martin Luther King Jr. Parade *(San Diego)*; Flight Day at Brown Field *(South County)*.

• February—The Chinese New Year celebration *(San Diego)*; a visit to Anza-Borrego State Park to see the wildflowers, the Vietnamese Tet Festival *(San Diego)*.

• March—The Ocean Beach Kite Festival *(San Diego)*, St. Patrick's Day Parade *(San Diego)*, the Pegleg Liar's Contest (Anza-Borrego State Park), César Chávez Day parade *(San Diego)*.

• April—Earth Fair (Balboa Park), Children's Day in the Park (Balboa Park), the Easter Hat Parade *(San Diego)*, local communities' Easter egg hunts.

• May—Cinco de Mayo festivities (multiple locations—see Appendix 1), Buds 'n Bloom festival in Balboa Park *(San Diego)*, Cupa Days Celebration on the Pala reservation *(North County Inland)*, free admission to the Wild Animal Park *(North County Inland)* on the second Wednesday in May.

• June—Corpus Christi Festival on the Pala reservation *(North County Inland)*, the Greek Festival *(San Diego)*, the Scottish Highland Games in San Marcos *(North County Inland)*, the Portuguese Festa *(San Diego)*, Clown Day in Julian *(North County Inland)*, and the Grunion Festival in Pacific Beach *(San Diego)*. See Appendix 1 for a list of the free concerts and the free cinemas that get started throughout the county as summer approaches.

• July—Festival of the Bells at Mission San Diego de Alcalá *(San Diego)*, the Pacific Islander Festival *(San Diego)*, the summer Organ Festival in Balboa Park *(San Diego)*, the Sand Castle Competition in Imperial Beach *(South County)*, the Obon Festival in Vista *(North County Inland)*.

• August—The Latin American Festival at the Bazaar del Mundo in Old Town *(San Diego)*, the Barona Barbecue on the Barona reservation *(East County)*, the Philippine Cultural Arts Festival in Balboa Park *(San Diego)*, the U.S. Navy's Fleet Week in *(San Diego)*.

• September—Mexican Independence Day celebrations in Old Town *(San Diego)* and in National City *(South County)*, California Indian Days Celebration in Balboa Park *(San Diego)*, the Cabrillo Festival *(San Diego)*, the Julian apple harvest in Julian *(North County Inland)*.

• October—Free admission for children at the Wild Animal Park *(North County Inland)* and the Zoo *(San Diego)* all month and free admission for everyone on the first Monday in October, the Miramar Air Show *(San Diego)*, the Cal State San Marcos Pow Wow *(North County Inland)*, Halloween celebrations at the Self Realization Fellowship in Encinitas *(North County Coastal)* and at Spreckels Park in Coronado *(South County)*.

• November—Celebration of the Day of the Dead in Old Town *(San Diego)*, Festival of Lights in Old Town *(San Diego)*, the Mother Goose Parade in El Cajon *(East County)*, the Santee Holiday Parade *(East County)*, the Starlight Yule Parade in Chula Vista *(South County)*.

• December—Christmas on the Prado in Balboa Park *(San Diego)*, Old Town's Las Posadas festivities *(San Diego)*, the Parades of Lights in the Harbors of Chula Vista *(South County)*, San Diego, Mission Bay *(San Diego)*, and Oceanside *(North County Coastal)*.

Adventures by Region

See individual chapters for details of each adventure.
See "How to Use This Book" for communities included in each region.

SAN DIEGO

Chapter 1: The Big Ones
- The Zoo
- SeaWorld

Chapter 2: Balboa Park
- All of the attractions in Balboa Park are in the San Diego region

Chapter 3: Beach and Bay Adventures
- All beaches and tide pools from La Jolla through Ocean Beach
- Mission Bay, Shelter Island, Harbor Island
- Crystal Pier, Shelter Island Pier, the Ocean Beach Pier
- The La Jolla caves
- The leopard sharks off of La Jolla Shores
- Seal Rock Marine Mammal Preserve
- All of the whale watching excursions except Helgrens

Chapter 4: Adventures in Parks and Lakes
- Fishing at Lake Miramar
- Fishing at Chollas Lake

Chapter 5: Adventures in Nature
- Torrey Pines State Park
- Bayside Trail at Cabrillo National Monument
- Famosa Slough
- Stephen Birch Aquarium and Museum
- "Nature in your Neighborhood" program at Chollas Park

Chapter 6: Adventures in Town
- Seaport Village
- Horton Plaza
- Bazaar del Mundo
- University Town Center
- Kobey's Swap Meet
- Zany Brainy, Learning Express, and Lakeshore Learning Center
- The Basic Brown Bear Factory
- Dr. Martin Luther King Jr. Promenade
- The tea party at the U.S. Grant Hotel
- Farmers' Markets (Hillcrest, Linda Vista, Mission Valley, Talmadge, Trolley Stop, Pacific Beach, Ocean Beach)
- The Bridges of San Diego County

Chapter 7: Adventures in Time
- Cabrillo National Monument
- Serra Museum
- Mission San Diego de Alcalá
- Old Town State Historic Park
- The Firehouse Museum

- The Maritime Museum
- The San Diego Historical Society Museum
- The Computer Museum

Chapter 8: Adventures of the Mind

- The Elementary Institute of Science
- Ruben H. Fleet Space Theater and Science Center Planetarium
- The Children's Museum/Museo de los Niños
- Stories, music, crafts, etc. at Zany Brainy, Lakeshore Learning Store, White Rabbit Children's Books, and all the Barnes & Noble and Borders Bookstores. Stories at all branches of the San Diego Public Library
- Drama opportunities at the Southeastern Community Theater, the J Company, the Christian Youth Theater, and San Diego Jr. Theater
- Musical opportunities at the San Diego Children's Choir, the Civic Youth Orchestra, the Youth Master Chorale, the Youth Symphony, and the San Diego Symphony's Youth Concerts, as well as the free pipe organ concerts in Balboa Park
- Classes at the Stephen Birch Aquarium, the San Diego Museum of Man, the San Diego Natural History Museum, the San Diego Humane Society, the San Diego Zoo, and SeaWorld
- Art classes at the San Diego Museum of Art, the Museum of Contemporary Art, the Athenaeum School of the Arts, the San Diego Art Institute, Art Tours, and various ceramics studios
- Crafts classes at Home Depot stores, Michael's stores, Ace Hardware stores, and Woodshop for Children
- Dance opportunities at Centro Cultural de la Raza and the WorldBeat Center

Chapter 9: Adventures of the Body

- Roller skating at Skate World and Rollerblade Blade School
- Skateboard Parks including the Washington Street Skate Park, Narrowgate Skate Park, and the Mission Valley YMCA Krause Family Skate Park
- Ice skating at the Ice Chalet and the San Diego Ice Arena
- Bicycling at Balboa Park, Mission Bay Park, Mission Beach Promenade, and more
- Horseback riding with Canyon Side Trail Rides
- Youth Tennis San Diego
- Pro Kids Golf Academy and the Junior Golf Association
- Rock climbing at the Vertical Hold Climbing Center and at Solid Rock
- Boating and water sports at Aqua Adventures Kayak School, Southwest Kayaks, Windsport Resort Watersports, Mission Bay Sportscenter, CP Watersports
- Deep sea fishing with all listed outfitters except Helgrens, which is in Oceanside
- Swimming at The Plunge, at any municipal pool, or with the Jr. Lifeguard program
- Team sports: Pop Warner football, Little League baseball, Youth Soccer Leagues; Classes with San Diego Padres' Camp for Kids, Valley Baseball School and Softball Academy, the Baseball Academy of San Diego State University, Randy Jones Baseball Academy, Allstar Baseball
- Spectator sports at Qualcomm Stadium, the San Diego Sports Arena, Douglas Stadium at Mesa College, and San Diego Chargers' Training Camp at UCSD, as well as the Buick Invitational Golf Tournament at Torrey Pines

Chapter 10: Excursions, Amusements, Tours

- Harbor Cruises
- The Coronado Ferry
- The San Diego Water Taxi
- The Gondola Company
- The San Diego Trolley
- Old Town Trolley Tours
- Amtrak and The Coaster
- Belmont Park
- Boomers
- Chuck E. Cheese
- Starworks
- Tours of SeaWorld, the San Diego Zoo, and the Navy Pier

Appendix 1: Adventures through the Year—Calendar of Annual Events

- January—Whale watching, Dr. Martin Luther King Jr. Parade, Teddy Bear, Doll, and Toy Festival
- February—Chinese New Year celebration, Vietnamese Tet Festival
- March—Ocean Beach Kite Festival, St. Patrick's Day parade, César Chávez Day parade
- April—EarthFair, Children's Day in the Park, Easter Week tea party at the Westgate Hotel
- May—Cinco de Mayo festivities, Buds 'n Bloom Kids Day, Dr. Seuss Kids' Magic Mile Run/Walk
- June—Indian Fair, Greek Festival, Portuguese Festa, Grunion Festival, start of summer specials including Tuesday discounts at Belmont Park, Movies Before the Mast on the Star of India, Saturday Movie Madness at the San Diego Public Library, Cinema Under the Stars at University Town Center, nighttime specials at the Zoo and at SeaWorld, La Jolla Concerts by the Sea
- July—Festival of the Bells at the San Diego Mission, Pacific Islander Festival, Summer Organ Festival
- August—Latin American Festival at the Bazaar del Mundo, Philippine Cultural Arts Festival, Fleet Week
- September—Mexican Independence Day fiesta in Old Town, California American Indian Day Celebration, Cabrillo Festival, Harbor Days
- October—Air Show at Miramar Marine Air Station, Children's month at the Zoo, Halloween celebrations and carnivals in Balboa Park and downtown San Diego
- November—Día de los Muertos celebration in Old Town, Festival of Lights in Old Town
- December—Christmas on the Prado, Old Town's Las Posadas, Balboa Park's museums' holiday events, Parade of Lights on Mission Bay and San Diego Harbor, First Night in San Diego

NORTH COUNTY COASTAL

Chapter 1: The Big Ones

- LEGOLAND

Chapter 2: Balboa Park

- No Balboa Park attractions in North County Coastal

Chapter 3: Beach and Bay Adventures

- All beaches and tide pools from Oceanside through Del Mar
- Pier fishing from Oceanside Pier

Chapter 4: Adventures in Parks and Lakes

- Guajome Regional Park
- San Dieguito County Park

Chapter 5: Adventures in Nature

- Quail Gardens
- North County Lagoons
- Weidner's Gardens

- Free Flight Aviary
- The Monarch Butterfly Program

Chapter 6: Adventures in Town

- Plaza Camino Real
- Oceanside Drive-in Swap Meet
- Seaside Bazaar and Cedros Ave. Jumble Flea Market
- Farmers' Markets in Oceanside, Carlsbad, Vista, Encinitas, Solana Beach, and Del Mar
- The Learning Express
- Knorr Candle Factory
- Aviara Four Seasons' afternoon tea

Chapter 7: Adventures in Time

- Mission San Luis Rey de Francia
- California Surf Museum
- The Museum of Making Music
- The Dinosaur Gallery
- Heritage Park Village and Museum
- San Dieguito Heritage Museum
- Antique Gas and Steam Engine Museum
- Vista Historical Museum/Rancho Adobe
- Rancho Guajome Adobe

Chapter 8: Adventures of the Mind

- Children's Discovery Museum
- Stories, crafts, music, etc. at The Learning Express, Barnes & Noble, Bookstar, Crown Books, and all public libraries
- Drama opportunities at the Moonlight Amphitheater, North County Repertory Company, San Diego Actors Theater, Christian Youth Theater
- Arts and crafts at Woodshop for Children, ceramics centers, Home Depot stores, Michael's Stores, and Ace Hardware stores.
- Classes at the Helen Woodward Animal Center

Chapter 9: Adventures of the Body

- Roller skating at Oceanside Roller Rink
- Skateboarding at the Magdalena Ecke Family YMCA and the Carlsbad Safety Center
- Bicycling in multiple locations; several bicycle rental shops available. Dirt Bike Haven at the Magdelena Ecke Family YMCA
- Adventure Ski and Snowboard School
- Water sports at Carlsbad Paddle Sports and California Watersports Rental
- Deep sea fishing with Helgrens
- Team sports including Pop Warner Football, Little League baseball, Youth Soccer; Baseball classes through Allstar Baseball.
- Spectator sports at the Carlsbad Raceway, San Diego Polo Club, and La Costa Resort's Toshiba Tennis Classic.

Chapter 10: Excursions, Amusements, Tours

- The Wave Water Park
- Amtrak and The Coaster
- Boomers
- Chuck E. Cheese
- McClellan-Palomar Airport tour
- Helen Woodward Animal Center

Appendix 1: Adventures through the Year—Annual Calendar of Events

- *Remember to check for local carnivals, festivals, street fairs, etc. in the* San Diego Family Magazine, San Diego Parent, *or the* San Diego Reader. *See Appendix 1 for details on finding these publications!*
- March—Junior Carlsbad Run
- April—Kids' Day at the Carlsbad Flower Fields
- May—Cinco de Mayo festivities at various locations

• June—Southern California Exposition (also known as the Del Mar Fair), Threshing Bee and Antique Engine Show, free summer concerts in multiple locations
• July—Del Mar horseracing (Family Days), Obon Festival
• September—Greek festival in Cardiff-by-the-Sea
• October—Halloween celebration at the Self Realization Fellowship in Encinitas (open to the public), Threshing Bee and Antique Engine Show
• November—Festival of Lights at the Del Mar Fairgrounds
• December—Quail Gardens Holiday events, Parade of Lights at Oceanside Harbor

NORTH COUNTY INLAND

Chapter 1: The Big Ones

• The Wild Animal Park

Chapter 2: Balboa Park

• No Balboa Park attractions in North County Inland

Chapter 3: Beach and Bay Adventures

• No beaches or bays in North County Inland

Chapter 4: Adventures in Parks and Lakes

• Dos Picos County Park
• Felicita County Park
• Live Oak Park
• Lake Hodges (for fishing)
• Lake Poway
• Dixon Lake

Chapter 5: Adventures in Nature

• Wilderness Gardens Preserve
• Daley Ranch Open Space Preserve

• Elfin Forest Recreational Preserve
• San Dieguito River Valley Park, including the Children's Interpretive Walk
• Blue Sky Ecologic Reserve
• Los Peñasquitos Canyon Preserve
• Bates Nut Farm
• Bell Gardens
• The Wildlife Rehabilitation Center
• Palomar Mountain
• Iron Mountain

Chapter 6: Adventures in Town

• Escondido Swap Meet
• Farmers' Markets in Borrego Springs, Escondido, Fallbrook, Julian, Poway, Rancho Bernardo
• The Learning Express

Chapter 7: Adventures in Time

• San Pasqual State Historic Park
• Julian
• Mission San Antonio de Pala, and Cupa Cultural Center
• Deer Park Winery and Auto Museum
• Escondido Historical Society's Heritage Walk
• Old Poway Park
• Ramona Pioneer Historical Society

Chapter 8: Adventures of the Mind

• Stories, crafts, music, etc. at The Learning Express, Barnes & Noble, Borders Books, Waldenbooks, and all public libraries
• Drama opportunities at the California Center for the Arts, the Patio Playhouse, the Poway Center for the Performing Arts, Christian Youth Theater, Broadway Bound Youth Theater
• Arts and crafts at ceramics centers, Home Depot stores, Michael's stores, Ace Hardware stores
• Palomar Observatory
• Palomar College Planetarium
• Classes at the Wild Animal Park

Chapter 9: Adventures of the Body

• Roller skating at the Ups-N-Downs Roller Rink
• Roller skating in the Garage (San Marcos)
• Skate boarding and roller hockey at the Escondido Sports Center
• Ice skating and ice hockey at the Iceoplex
• Horseback riding at Julian Stables Trail Rides
• Rock climbing at the Solid Rock Gym
• Swimming at all municipal pools and Las Posas Aquatic Center
• Team sports including Pop Warner football, Little League baseball, Youth Soccer leagues
• Paintball at Hidden Valley Paintball; Laser tag at the Poway Entertainment Center

Chapter 10: Excursions, Amusement, Tours

• Sengeme Oaks Water Park
• The Stewart Gem Mine
• The Eagle and High Peak Mines
• Boomers
• Chuck E. Cheese
• Nickel City
• Tours at the Wild Animal Park
• The Poway Entertainment Center

Appendix 1: Adventures through the Year—Annual Calendar of Events

• *Remember to check for local carnivals, festivals, street fairs, etc. in the* San Diego Family Magazine, San Diego Parent, *or the* San Diego Reader. *See Appendix 1 for details on finding these publications!*
• February—Wildflowers bloom in Anza-Borrego State Park, Fishing Derby at Lake Poway
• March—Pegleg Liars' Contest in Anza-Borrego State Park, Arbor Day at the Wild Animal Park

• May—Founders' Day at the Wild Animal Park (free admission), Cinco de Mayo festivities in Grape Day Park in Escondido, Cupa Days Celebration, the Ramona Round-Up
• June—Corpus Christi Fiesta, Scottish Highland Games, Clown Day, start of Wild Animal Park's summer night programs
• September—Apple harvest in Julian, Poway Rodeo
• October—Pumpkins and other Halloween attractions at Bates Nut Farm and Bell Garden; Pow Wow at Cal State San Marcos
• December—Festival of Lights at the Wild Animal Park, First Night in Escondido

EAST COUNTY

Chapter 1: The Big Ones

• None of the attractions in this section are in East County

Chapter 2: Balboa Park

• No Balboa Park attractions in East County

Chapter 3: Beach and Bay Adventures

• No beaches or bays in East County

Chapter 4: Adventures in Parks and Lakes

• Flinn Springs County Park
• Louis Seltzer Park
• Lake Murray and Mission Trails Regional Park
• San Vicente (fishing)
• Santee Lakes
• Lake Jennings
• Lake Moreno
• Lindo Lake
• Lake Cuyamaca

Chapter 5: Adventures in Nature

- Mission Trails Regional Park
- Mast Park
- Cuyamaca Rancho State Park
- Silverwood Wildlife Sanctuary

Chapter 6: Adventures in Town

- The Viejas Outlet Center
- Swap Meets in Spring Valley and Santee
- Farmers' Markets in Alpine, El Cajon, and La Mesa

Chapter 7: Adventures in Time

- The San Diego Railroad Museum
- The Gaskill Stone Store and Museum
- The Motor Transport Museum
- Heritage of the Americas Museum
- The "Spirit of Nightfire" at Viejas
- The Barona Museum and Cultural Center
- The Lakeside Historical Society
- The Bancroft Ranch House Museum
- The Air Force WWII Museum

Chapter 8: Adventures of the Mind

- Stories, crafts, music, etc. at Zany Brainy, The Yellow Book Road, Barnes & Noble, Bookstar, and all public libraries
- Drama opportunities at Christian Youth Theater, and El Cajon Summer Stock
- Arts and crafts at ceramics studios, Home Depot stores, Michael's stores, and Ace Hardware stores
- The Mount Laguna telescope

Chapter 9: Adventures of the Body

- Roller skating at La Mesa Sports Center, Parkway Sports Center, and Rollerskateland
- Horseback riding at Holidays on Horseback in the Cuyamaca mountains
- Fishing lessons at Lake Cuyamaca

- Laser tag at Laser Storm; paintball at Borderland Paintball Park
- Team sports including Pop Warner football, Little League baseball, and Youth Soccer Leagues
- Spectator sports at the El Cajon Speedway
- Skateboarding at Woodglen Vista Skate Park

Chapter 10: Excursions, Amusements, Tours

- San Diego Railroad Museum train excursions
- Boomers
- Chuck E. Cheese
- Tour of a Waste Management facility

Appendix 1: Adventures through the Year—Calendar of Annual Events

- *Remember to check for local carnivals, festivals, street fairs, etc. in the* San Diego Family Magazine, San Diego Parent, *or the* San Diego Reader. *See Appendix 1 for details on finding these publications!*
- April—Lakeside Western Days and Rodeo
- June—Free concerts on the Green in El Cajon
- October—Oktoberfest in El Cajon
- November—Mother Goose Parade, holiday parade in Santee

SOUTH COUNTY

Chapter 1: The Big Ones

- None of the attractions in this section are in South County

Chapter 2: Balboa Park

- No Balboa Park attractions in South County

More Adventures with Kids in San Diego

Chapter 3: Beach and Bay Adventures

- All beaches and bays in Coronado, and the beaches in Imperial Beach
- Pier fishing in Imperial Beach

Chapter 4: Adventures in Parks and Lakes

- Sweetwater County Park
- Otay Lakes

Chapter 5: Adventures in Nature

- Tijuana Estuary National Reserve
- The Chula Vista Nature Interpretive Center
- The Stein Family Farm

Chapter 6: Adventures in Town

- Chula Vista Shopping Center
- Swap Meets at Kobey's Marketplace and the National City Swap Meet
- Farmers' Markets in Chula Vista and Coronado

Chapter 7: Adventures in Time

- Hotel del Coronado
- Sweetwater-Rohr Park Railroad
- Kimball House
- Bonita Museum and Cultural Center

Chapter 8: Adventures of the Mind

- Stories, crafts, music, etc. at all public libraries
- Drama opportunities at Lamb's Players Theater
- Arts and crafts at ceramics studios, Home Depot stores, Michael's stores, Ace Hardware stores.
- Classes at the Chula Vista Nature Center

Chapter 9: Adventures of the Body

- Roller skate at Rollerskate Land and Skate San Diego
- Skateboard at Bored Bored? Skate Park and Andy A. Rogers Skate Park
- Horseback ride at Sandi's Rental Stables and at Sweetwater Farms
- Team sports including Pop Warner football, Little League baseball, Youth League soccer
- Spectator sports at the ARCO U.S. Olympic Training Center

Chapter 10: Excursions, Amusements, Tours

- Knott's Soak City USA Water Park
- Chuck E. Cheese
- Fun-4-All
- The Discovery Zone
- Tours at the ARCO U.S. Olympic Training Center

Appendix 1: Adventures through the Year—Annual Calendar of Events

- Remember to check for local carnivals, festivals, street fairs, etc. in the *San Diego Family Magazine, San Diego Parent*, or the *San Diego Reader*. See Appendix 1 for details on finding these publications!
- May—Cinco de Mayo festivities in Chula Vista, National City's Maytime Band Review Parade
- June—Free concerts in the park in Chula Vista
- July—Sand castle competition in Imperial Beach
- September—Mexican Independence Day festivities in Kimball Park
- November—Starlight Yule Parade in Chula Vista
- December—Parade of Lights in Chula Vista Harbor

196

Index

More Adventures with Kids in San Diego

More Adventures with Kids in San Diego

SUNBELT PUBLICATIONS
"Adventures in the Natural and Cultural History of the Californias"
Series Editor—Lowell Lindsay

San Diego Series:

Rise and Fall of San Diego: 150 Million Years	Abbott
More Adventures with Kids in San Diego	Botello, Paxton
Geology of San Diego: Journeys Through Time	Clifford, Bergen, Spear
Mission Trails Regional Park Trail Map	Cook
San Diego Mountain Bike Guide	Greenstadt
San Diego Specters: Ghosts, Poltergeists, Tales	Lamb
Discover San Diego, 16th Ed.	Peik
A Good Camp: Mines of Julian and the Cuyamacas	Fetzer
Campgrounds of San Diego County	Tyler
Portrait of Paloma: A Novel	Crosby

Southern California Series:

Campgrounds of Santa Barbara and Ventura Counties	Tyler
Campgrounds of Los Angeles and Orange Counties	Tyler
Mission Memoirs: Reflections on California's Past	Ruscin
California's El Camino Real and Its Historic Bells	Kurillo, Tuttle
Orange County: A Photographic Collection	Hemphill

California Desert Series:

Anza-Borrego A To Z: People, Places, and Things	D. Lindsay
Geology of the Imperial /Mexicali Valleys—SDAG 1998	L. Lindsay ed.
Palm Springs Oasis: A Photographic Essay	Lawson
Desert Lore of Southern California, 2nd Ed.	Pepper
Geology of Anza-Borrego: Edge of Creation, 2nd Ed.	Remeika, Lindsay
Paleontology of Anza-Borrego—SDAG 1995	Remeika, Sturz eds.
California Desert Miracle: Parks and Wilderness	Wheat

Baja California Series:

Cave Paintings of Baja California, Rev. Ed.	Crosby
Geology Terms in English and Spanish	Aurand
The Other Side: Journeys in Baja California	Botello
Backroad Baja: The Central Region	Higginbotham
Journey with A Baja Burro	Mackintosh
Sea of Cortez Review	Redmond
Houses of Los Cabos	Amaroma
Baja Legends: Historic Characters, Events, Locations	Niemann

Sunbelt books celebrate the land and its people through publications in natural science, outdoor adventure, and regional interest.